Raymond Cazallis Davis

Reminiscences of a Voyage Around the World

Raymond Cazallis Davis

Reminiscences of a Voyage Around the World

ISBN/EAN: 9783337190736

Printed in Europe, USA, Canada, Australia, Japan

Cover: Foto ©Andreas Hilbeck / pixelio.de

More available books at **www.hansebooks.com**

REMINISCENCES

OF A

VOYAGE

AROUND THE WORLD.

By R. C. DAVIS,

Assistant Librarian in the University of Michigan.

ANN ARBOR, MICHIGAN:
DR. CHASE'S STEAM PRINTING HOUSE, 41 & 43 NORTH MAIN STREET.
1869.

PREFACE.

MANY young aspirants for literary honors represent their first literary productions as accidents, or occurrences as inevitable as fate. If you believe what they tell, you will think they were but faintly conscious of any voluntary act. They felt (they say) the throes of intellectual travail; sympathising friends called in the accoucheur (an accommodating publisher); then followed an interval of blank oblivion, after which they languidly raised themselves, and beheld, with emotions of profound surprise, the result, viz.: a 12mo, muslin covered volume!

All this is a diffuse way of presenting a view of the matter that "Wemmick" (a character of Dickens, remarkable for his idolatry of "portable property," and the numerous *accidents* that befel him,) would have presented in the single exclamation, "Halloo, here's a book!"

This little volume was produced in no such miraculous way. It was written for the purpose of increasing, to something like an adequate amount, an insufficient salary. The labor was often done in weariness and depression.

It is not expected that mature minds will find, either in the style or the matter, much to interest or instruct them. But it *is* hoped that for boys, this narrative of youthful experience, on the "great ocean," and in "distant lands," will possess interest, and afford instruction.

POSSESS INTEREST—because there is something irresistible to youth in the weird charms of the ocean, laving, as it does, the shores of so many and such diverse lands; reflecting, the constellations of both hemispheres; and containing in its vast bosom such myriads of wonderful creatures.

AFFORD INSTRUCTION—because it is a faithful narrative of actual events, and describes truthfully the places visited during the voyage, as well as the habits of the people, so far as I had opportunity for observing them. Whatever interests and instructs, also exerts and influence. Now all influences are not for good. The moral scale in human experience, alas! is graded down as well as up. Have I thought of this? Yes, I realize the responsibility of one who would apply force to character. And I think there is not a thought expressed in all the following pages, that is inconsistent with this profession.

I should do violence to my feelings if I closed these prefaratory remarks, without saying that I feel towards the publisher of this volume, such sentiments as a grateful man feels towards him who has used him kindly and generously.

PUBLISHER'S NOTICE.

"I have heard of the far-off sea,
    I have heard of its hollow roar—
Of its rolling, rumbling revelry,
    Far out from the quiet shore;
I have heard of its caverns strange
        And deep,
Where the beings that heed no change,
        Find sleep."

WHO has not "heard of the far-off sea," and who, I would ask, is not deeply interested in all that relates to it? Probably there is no other subject of thought in the world, which so enchains the mind, of every reader, as a good description of sea-life incidents. Why such an interest in sea-life? Because the degree of interest awakened in the mind always depends upon the suddenness with which danger to human life may arise from the surrounding circumstances, and the means at hand, upon which one must depend for relief—rocky shores—sunken reefs—raging storms the lightning flash, etc., have all to be met, on the sea, and provided for at once, or destruction overwhelms them in a moment; and sometimes the danger is increased by the drunkenness or neglect of officers; for instance—the good ship Hampton has been running, one afternoon, with a light breeze, having all sails set, and the wind, at night, although somewhat changeable, yet not sufficiently so to shorten sail during the captain's watch, he having charged the mate to carefully observe the darkening sky, at the North, during his watch, and, if need be, "to unreeve the studding-sail gear, rig in the booms, and furl the light sails;" but instead of keeping "an eye" on the clouds, he allowed them to close in sleep, until the dawn of the morning, when the captain, realizing a change in the atmosphere, jumped out of bed to consult the barometer, and finding that it had fallen alarmingly, hastened to the deck to find the mate just waking from his stolen slumbers, rubbing his eyes, and not yet half awake: while "a glance aloft showed that he had neglected his orders. The studding-sail booms were out, the gear all rove, and all sail set, from the flying jib to the spanker—from the royals to the deck; and just to windward, close aboard, was a furious squall bearing down upon the ship. Before it, on the water, a line of white foam—above, a black impenatrable wall, reaching to the frantically flying clouds."

The captain, realizing the danger of his position, sings out, in a stentorian voice, to the mate—"Go below, sir. Go directly below, sir!—hard up your wheel—work sharp! Call all hands. Clew up the royals and topgallant-sails, fore and aft. Down flying jib and stay-sails. Brail up the spanker," etc.,—which put every man upon duty in the ship, the neglectful mate excepted, with all the activity they were master of, to save themselves from immediate destruction by the fury of the storm. Upon another occasion a man jumped over-board in a storm, and was lost, etc., ect.

Think you, gentle reader, that there was *no interest* felt by those on board the Hampton, under these circumstances? Or, where can you find an individual, old or young, who can read the description of these incidents, without having his whole soul thrilled with an intensity of interest, as though actually suffering with them in their imminent peril?

PUBLISHER'S NOTICE.

This voyage was made in a new merchant ship, the "Hampton," from Bath, Maine, between September, 1849 and August, 1851, via Cape Horn to San Francisco, and the Sandwich and other Islands of the Western Pacific, to Calcutta, returning by the Cape of Good Hope to London, England, thence to Boston, touching at many intermediate points along the route, in the Western Pacific, East Indies, etc., of which no previous description has been given.

And this voyage undoubtedly proved more full of interesting incidents from the fact, as will be seen from the above dates, that it was made in the time of the California "gold fever;" hence, most of the crew left the ship at San Francisco for the gold fields, and others could only be shipped to go as far as the Sandwich Islands, from which place only raw "Kanakas"—Sandwich Islanders—could be obtained, among whom ignorance, neglect of duty, and mutiny were the most prominent traits of character, calling for instruction, great patience, and, upon one occasion, the handcuffs, "to bring them to time."

The Author being also a son of the captain, whose life had been spent upon the ocean, a much better chance for observation was enjoyed, and a much greater amount of information received, than would have been obtained by any other writer.

The "Reminiscences" were first written for the "Youths' Department" of the PENINSULAR COURIER AND FAMILY VISITANT, a weekly newspaper we have published some five years, the readers of which, old as well as young, clergymen as well as others, have called for their publication in book form; therefore, notwithstanding the natural timidity of the author, leads him to say: "It is not expected that *mature* minds will find, either in the *style* or the *matter*, much to interest or instruct them, hoping, only, that the narrative will possess interest and instruction for boys;" yet, the publisher, taking it for granted that what has greatly interested the *mature* readers of the COURIER AND VISITANT will also interest all other readers, has deemed their publication, in book form, advisable; hence, they have been revised by the writer—adding a few incidents which memory had brightened and burnished by dwelling upon them, after the first writing—making the work, no doubt, one of the most useful and interesting books, of the kind, before the people—*blending interest with historical instruction to such an extent that every reader will be profited by its perusal.*

With these remarks and explanations, therefore, the publisher has, most cheerfully, undertaken to place the "Reminiscences of a Voyage Around the World," in a permanent form, before the reading public.

A. W. CHASE.

ANN ARBOR, MICH., August, 1869.

CONTENTS.

CHAPTER I.

At Bath.—Destination the "Golden Gate," San Francisco.—Slushing down the mast.—"So you are the Captain's Son, are you?"—The "ship's cousin."

CHAPTER II

"Out to sea."—Jackknife Ledge.—Heartsick, homesick, and *sea-sick*.—Instruction to those seeking "a life on the ocean wave, and a home on the rolling deep."—A new existence, after the sea-sickness.—A consciousness of the presence of God.—On Him the trusting heart leans daily.

CHAPTER III.

The Gulf Stream.—What makes it?—Different theories.—Its course and benefits.

CHAPTER IV.

The Ship, her crew, and something concerning her management; or, sea-usages.

CHAPTER V.

Sickness and death of Ezra Whitman.—He committed his frail bark to Christ, the faithful Pilot and Steward, for that city whose twelve gates are twelve pearls, and whose streets are of pure gold.—A comparison.—A burial at sea, and seamen's superstitions.

CHAPTER VI.

The "Sargasso," or weedy sea, interesting to the naturalist, classical, and mediæval student.—Yellow-covered literature, or "dime novels."—To cure the propensity for reading them.

CHAPTER VII.

The Trade Winds.—Their study increases our love and reverence for the Great Creator.—Phosphorescent light in the ship's path.—"A man overboard."—The old Spanish navigators.—The poetry of the sea.—The Dolphin, Petrel, Porpoise, Nautilus and Tropic Birds.

CHAPTER VIII.

The calms of the Equator, the sailors' "*Doldrums.*"—Intense heat.—Poor water.—Capture of a Shark.—Lifted on deck.—The "Doctor" prostrated by a blow from its caudal extremity.—Like the opossum, the female shark, when in danger, secures its young within itself.—Different species.—Perpetual summer.—The Sun is king.—Rare beauty of a tropical "sunset at sea."

CHAPTER IX.

The Island of Fernando Noronha, the Van Dieman's Land of Brazil.—A suspicious sail.—Sailors prepare for a fight.—Off Cape Frio.—Catamaran, the Brazilian craft for trading and coasting.—Arrival at Rio Janeiro.

CHAPTER X.

A description of Rio Janeiro and its surroundings.—The American Consul, Ex-Gov. Kent, of Maine, dines on board the Hampton.—The Chigoe, beds in your flesh.—Lizards, cockroaches and snakes get into the bed.—Scorpions sting on the foot.—Everything bites, stings, or bruises in the Tropics.

CHAPTER XI.

A Jesuit experiments with the Chigoe; *but loses his foot.*—Empire of Brazil.—Start from Rio.—"The Brazilians are brave."

CHAPTER XII.

Tropical Birds and Fishes.—The Booby, so called from its tameness or indifference to capture.—Lieut. Bligh and his companions set adrift in mid-ocean by the mutineers of the Bounty, were saved from starvation by the capture of this bird, (See Chap. XXII for the end of his voyage).—Frigate-bird.—Flying-fish, etc.—The "Doctor." (cooks, on shipboard, are always called "Doctor.")—Loses his "free papers" at Rio.—A passenger finds and returns them.

CHAPTER XIII.

A heavy gale.—Bird-catching.—The Albatross.—The Stormy Petrel, from Peter, because they walk on the water.—The Dogfish.—Fall in with the Harriet Rockwell, from Boston, and the Oriental, from Machias, Me., full of passengers, bound for the golden shores of California.—Visit, and sail on together.

CHAPTER XIV.

A trial of speed.—The Hampton outsails all competitors.—Enter Valparaiso, Chili.—Description of the bay and city.—A street fight, while there, between the Police and about 200 English and American men-of-war's men.—One Policeman killed.—Great excitement.—An explanation about the loss of the Essex, Com. Porter, at this place, in the last war with England, Admiral Farragut participating as midshipman.—French passengers from Valparaiso to San Francisco.—One, a Conjurer.—Some of his tricks.—Nearly a fight.—Reach the "Golden Gate," San Francisco, Feb. 27, 1850, 173 days out.—Eldorado at last, and out of seventy souls, all there save two, Whitman and the Steward, who jumped overboard in a storm.

CHAPTER XV.

Bay of San Francisco.—Forests of masts.—Ships from every land.—The Golden Gate, entrance to the Bay.—Islands de los Angeles, Los Aleatrazes, and Yerba Buena.—Currents of the Pacific.—Mate and Steward discharged, and the crew run off to the "gold diggin's."—Cargo discharged.—Ship chartered to go to Calcutta and load for London.—Crew shipped for the Sandwich Islands.—Sansalito.—Mrs. Brown.—Sail for Honolulu.

CHAPTER XVI.

Arrive at Honolulu.—Sailors leave to return to San Francisco.—They constitute our Author their Treasurer while they visit the shore.—A sailor's economy.—Description of the Island.—The Missionary work, and what they had to contend with.

CHAPTER XVII.

Still at Honolulu.—Further description.—The Devil's Punch Bowl, the crater of an extinct volcano.—A Kanaka crew.

CHAPTER XVIII.

Description of our Kanaka crew.—Sail from Honolulu.—Violent rolling of the ship.—Awkwardness and fright of the Kanakas.—The Cook calls them to account for wasting his beans; "If dat's de way de beans go, dar wont be many board dis ship before soon."—Instructing the Kanakas to work the ship.—The Gillolo and Ombay passage chosen, through which to pass the East Indian Archipelago.

CHAPTER XIX.

In the Torrid Zone.—Illness of the Author.—Burning thirst, and not allowed water.—Tantalizing dreams of water.—Recovery.—Independence Day, off the Ladrones.—Fire the brass four-pounder.—The Mate kicks a Kanaka.—Mutiny.—Five whites and one colored, the cook, against nine Kanakas.—Ladron is a Spanish word signifying a thief or a robber, the disposition of the inhabitants of the Ladrones.

CHAPTER XX.

The Island of Mariere, near the Molucca Passage.—Contrary winds. "Swinging round the circle."—In sight of the Island thirteen days.—*Miserere*, a more appropriate name.—Gained a day by sailing west.—Explanation, by Edgar A. Poe, of "Three Sabbaths in one week."—Passing the Molucca Passage.—Island of Gillolo, one of the largest of the Moluccas, or Spice Islands.—Productions.—Belongs to the Dutch.—Reptiles, "Birds of Paradise, etc.—Malay conquerors.—Treacherous and bloodthirsty.—Bouro Dome, or Tamahoe Mountain.—The Doctor's difficulty to make one of the Kanaka crew understand him.—Strength of the Kanaka's skull.—Tougher than a squash.

CHAPTER XXI.

Becalmed under the shadow of Bouro Dome, on the Island of Xulla Bessy.—Squally.—Fearful of the coast of Celebes.—A sail.—Copang, on the Island of Timor, chosen to stop at for water.—The "Milky Sea."—Report of Capt. Trebuchat, of the corvette Capricieuse, through the French Minister of Marine, to the Academy of Science, in Paris, as to its cause.—Attributed to glow-worm animalculæ.—A blow with an iron belaying pin upon a Kanaka's skull.—A Kanaka again in irons.—Rocky Island of Po Cambing.—In sight of Copang.—A schooner leads us into the Bay.

CHAPTER XXII.

At Copang.—Meet the captain of the New Bedford whale-ship Phœnix.—Copang celebrated for the hospitalities shown Lieut. Bligh and his companions on their remarkable open-boat voyage, forty-seven days out, sailed 3,600 miles, the work of mutineers, (see Chap. XII).—Obtain water.—Monkeys.—Description of Copang and the Island.—Poultry and vegetables plenty.—Malays piratical.—To "run a-muck."

CHAPTER XXIII.

A deserter from the Phœnix on board.—Taken back.—Desperate case.—Depart from Copang.—Indian Ocean.—Java Head.—Sailors' sports on board.—Furious squall.—Ship down on her broadside, fearfully.—Rain in torrents.—Kanakas useless in the rigging.—A toilsome night.—A Kanaka falls through a hatchway, twenty feet, strikes his head on an anchor, knocking off a bit of scalp only.—How thick his skull?—Had he any brains?

CHAPTER XXIV.

Fretful weather.—A chafing, vexing, wearying morning, after a laborious night.—A whirlwind and waterspouts endanger the ship.—"There seemed no possibility of escape."—"The Unseen Hand was again stretched out."—The appalling danger overbalanced by the awful sublimity of the scene.—Reach the Bay of Bengal.—Monstrous turtles.—"A Paddy's box of snakes."—The monkeys on board imitate the men.—Enter the Hoogly.—Reach Calcutta.—Oppressive atmosphere.—A gang of Lascars employed to do duty on board.—The Hindoo abominates swine's flesh equal to the Jew.—They live on rice.—Not equal in strength to the sailors.—The Hoogly the chief, or largest mouth of the Ganges.—Description.—Dead bodies on the river.

CHAPTER XXV.

Still at Calcutta, called the "City of Palaces," as properly the "City of Mud Huts."—Dining with the American Consul, chickens, rice and *curry*.—Our Author tries it and thinks it "*some*."—His health fails in this climate.—The Doctor has "a round" with a Kanaka, who is put in irons, the captain arrives in time to save a fight with all the Kanakas.—The Kanaka dies of fever.—All the other Kanakas, except one, run off, giving much joy in the ship.—A Hindoo sharper.—Mate discharged.

CHAPTER XXVI.

Still at Calcutta.—Another mate discharged for drunkenness.—Jugglers.—"See snakee dance."—Religious holidays.—The cargo all on board.—Departure from Calcutta.—Another drunken mate.—Off Sangor Island New Year's Day, 1851.—"Splicing the main brace."—New crew, mostly Scotchmen.—After getting to sea the Author's health recruits again.—Feb. 17, off Madagascar.—Cape of Good Hope not, as generally supposed, the most southern point of Africa.—Cape Lagullus 20 miles south of it.

CONTENTS.

CHAPTER XXVII.

Pass the Cape of Good Hope, called by Capt. Diaz, *Cabo Tormentoso*, the Cape of Storms.—Comparison with Cape Horn.—Smooth sailing.—Every sail set "alow and aloft."—"Yarning and caulking."—St. Helena in sight, March 18.—Anchor off Jamestown, before sunset.—The Island narrow but lofty.—Jamestown, Ladder Hill and High Knoll make a *two story* mountain, in the rear, over 2,000 feet high.—Diana's Peak 2,700.—Fortifications, etc.—Good mackerel fishing at the Island.—Fresh mackerel better than salt beef.—The discovery of the Island, 1501.—Description.—Many vessels at the Island.—Sail in company with a whaler, the Corinthian.—A dangerous squall and a sleepy mate.—The "Sargasso Sea," again.—Pass the Azores.—Becalmed near an English brig.—Receive the first information of the Crystal Palace at London, and the high expectations of it.— "Good," exclaim all hands, "we shall be there just in the right time."—Reach the English Channel in the night.—Meet an English brig and enquire, "What light?"—Answer, "The *Heddystone*."—"What time of tide?"—"'Igh water," is answered.

CHAPTER XXVIII.

Arrival at London.—Custom-House officers short of pocket handkerchiefs, so they take the "Doctor's," bought for Mrs. Brown, in Calcutta.—Ship discharges cargo, and loads with iron and chalk for Boston.—Walk outside of London.—Run down the Straits of Dover.—"The White Cliffs of Albion."—Tornado on the land while off Medford, Waltham and West Cambridge.—A Dutch sailor thinks "De blixen! Mein Gott, I dinks de end of de world pe come!"—A quick run to Boston.—The "Goodbyes."—The Author's "best bow."

REMINISCENCES

OF A

VOYAGE AROUND THE WORLD.

CHAPTER I.

AT BATH.

NOT "Ba—ath," in *old* England, the home of Beau Nash, the "Aquæ Solis"—waters of the Sun—of the Romans, to which place "Angelo Cyrus Bantum, Esq., M. C.," welcomed Mr. Pickwick so cordially, but a more youthful city, Bath on the River Kennebec, in *new* England, a city whose ships navigate every sea, and every other one of whose inhabitants is a captain or a mate.

Thither, to join the ship Hampton, my brother and myself, one morning early in August, 1849, sailed from our home at the mouth of the Georges River, in a little centre-board sloop, bearing the euphonic name of "Horse and Buggy." An uncle and a cousin were with us, who were charged with our safe delivery.

There was a fresh breeze from the North, and the little sloop, carrying a huge "bone in her mouth," soon rounded Pemmaquid Point, and then my uncle, who was pilot, and a veritable Palinurus, by the way, hauled his wind, and skirting the breakers on Thrum Cap, ran over to the eastern entrance to Townsend Thoroughfare. From thence, our way was through a devious inland passage.

Sometimes we would run, with sheet off, down a narrow strait, a salt marsh within toss of a biscuit, on either hand, and then suddenly dart out into a broad bay where fleets might manœuvre.

Having crossed this, our course would change, and we would *beat* through another strait, equally as narrow as the former one, but with high, rocky banks, covered with huckleberry bushes. Through this the tide would be running with us, like the sluice-way of a mill, and the "Horse and Buggy" would forereach as she went in stays, like an arrow shot from a bow.

Under all circumstances we made good progress, and the sun was hardly set when we entered the Kennebec, opposite Bath, and saw the white ports of the Hampton across the river.

The Hampton was a new ship, registering 443 tons, old tonnage, and built that summer at Richmond, a few miles above Bath, on the river. She was advertised, of course, and the advertisement ran like this:

"FOR SAN FRANCISCO.—The Letter A, No. 1, coppered, copper-fastened, and fast-sailing ship Hampton, ——— Master, will have immediate dispatch, as above.

"For freight, or passage, apply immediately, &c., &c."

This advertisement was not incorrect above all others, yet I can see where it was open to criticism. Canvass had never been spread upon the ship. How could it be known, then, that she was fast-sailing? And I wonder if the bolts used in fastening a ship are all counted, and if it is only when the copper ones far outnumber the iron ones, that the ship is said to be copper-fastened? But what are advertisements for!

The ship was receiving lumber for her cargo. To carry lumber to San Francisco now would be "carrying coals to Newcastle," but it was not so then, and enormous freights were paid.

The lading of the ship went briskly on, but not carelessly, for I never saw space so economized anywhere, before or since. Bunches of shingles were opened, and wherever one could be driven, there one was put. I did not play a very important part in anything. An anecdote will explain my status.

One day a second mate was shipped and entered upon his duties. After examining the condition of things aloft, he concluded to have the masts slushed down. At that moment I was the only available person in sight. He therefore ordered me to take a slush bucket, go up to the main royal mast, and give that, and the topgallant mast and topmast, a coat of grease. I complied so far as to take a bucket and climb up into the topmast crosstrees. Further I could not go. It was in vain that I twisted my legs around the rigging and exerted all my strength to ascend. Although only thirteen years of age, I was nearly six feet in height, and my frame was large and heavy. But on account of severe injuries received in the chest, my strength was at that time inversely as the length of my limbs and the size of my body. After several vain efforts, I made the bucket fast to the rigging, and descended.

"Well?" said the officer, enquiringly, as I stepped upon the deck.

"I made the bucket fast," I answered, glancing aloft at it. "I couldn't get clear up."

"You *couldn't*, hey?" he said, in a tone in which wrath was very perceptible. "Well, you just try it again."

"I shan't," I answered, "for it's no use."

"You *shan't*," he roared, looking at me from head to foot, with anger and curiosity in his eyes. "Look here, my lad, men don't say *shan't* when they're afloat. I shall report your case to the captain."

"Well," I answered, "I don't think father would send me where I couldn't go."

"W-h-e-w!" He gave a prolonged whistle, and ejaculating, "So you're the captain's son, are you?" turned on his heel and left me.

I *was* the captain's son. Therefore, being the "ship's cousin," as the captain's relatives are termed afloat, and in a measure an invalid, I was privileged to be in the way a great deal, but not obliged to work much. And it really gave me opportunities for observation that I could not otherwise have possessed.

I have already intimated that we were bound for San Francisco. And this was not a solitary instance of a vessel loading for that port. All along our Atlantic sea-board, from Calais to New Orleans, every description of navigation was up for that same destination.

The old idea that had so long obtained, that none but the stoutest ships could round Cape Horn, was cast to the winds. Stout ships, indeed, there were, and many of them, preparing for the voyage. But there were others of a very different character —old, and unsound in hull and spars—that were eagerly purchased, or chartered. Freight and passengers poured into them, and when all was ready, their prows were pointed southward, and they were urged along by all the methods that the ingenuity of man could devise.

And the modern coaster, that all her days had been contented to hug the coast along, never aspiring to foreign voyages, or the unbounded sea, was suddenly launched upon this river of commotion, whose only issue was the route to California. Forthwith her worthy skipper reached from its shelf his long neglected Bowditch's Epitome, brushed from its covers the accumulated dust, and, out of its inestimable contents, renewed his navigation. Forth from its box he took his ancient quadrant; along the graduated scale moved the index, and squinted again through its ample sight vanes.

Good-bye to green water, nightly harbors, and the ever recurring course from headland to headland Hail to the blue, unsounded sea, a constant course, and Ophir—*surely Ophir*—for a destination.

In this fast age, the discovery of gold in California has become an antiquated event. But no event, at all recent, save the great Rebellion, has so thrilled the nation, or led to greater results.

Wealth and Adventure—why, these two combined are irresistible—irresistible to care-worn manhood, irresistible to dreamy youth! History records the triumphs of this temptation, and the instances are countless.

Now, its peculiar features were slightly changed. It was not the coin of any realm, nor the barbaric ornaments of either India. In no wise was it in the inventory of "Miss Killmansegg with the Precious Leg"—not

"———gold,
Molten, graven, hammered and rolled,"

but it was virgin ore, dust in the dust, and veins in the rock.

Who does not know how it was found? On the wings of the wind the tale flew eastward. As when the news of Lexington and Concord passed along the land, men suspended their labors, so now, when this tale of wealth ran from house to house, rolling like a subtile vapor up over mountains, and down into valleys, men paused from their occupations.

It was whispered in the room of the manufacturer, and that whisper was heard above the whirring of belt and the jarring of wheels; and the sounds ceased, for the tale was seductive and the manufacturer was seduced away.

The midnight air, as it floated through the dark streets of great cities, and eddied in and out of their subterranean dens, breathed the tale. And discordant music ceased, and unsightly dances ended. The inebriate forgot his full cup, and the murderer turned with bloodless knife from the clutched throat of his victim. The tale was seductive and they were seduced away.

The morning paper published the discovery, and

the pale clerk laid down his yard-stick, and the book-keeper closed his books. Lawyers cast Blackstone and Kent to dust and oblivion, and the sons of Esculapius compounded pills no more.

The weekly paper rehearsed the story of the daily. Mute grew the fisherman's fog horns by the shores of Maine, and on the land the fences fell unheeded, and where strong men had labored, children wrought their childish task. Around many doors the weeds, untrod, grew rank and tall, and within no fire warmed the cold hearths.

Oh! the tale *was* seductive, and many men were seduced away.

Across the Atlantic they came, too, from the old world, men in whom, by reason of oppression, hope was dead, yet avarice survived.

Many keels disturbed the waters of the Pacific, all pointing toward the Golden Gate. And the ships bore convicts from New South Wales, Lascars from India, and Chinese from the Celestial Empire.

How they thronged to the Land of Gold—all races, creeds and colors, the generous, the noble, the sordid and the mean.

CHAPTER II.

SEA-SICKNESS.

WHEN our state of preparation would admit of its being done with any degree of certainty, a day was fixed for sailing. It was the eighth day of September. And on that day, at 3 P. M., the ship, having on board, besides a cargo of lumber, a large quantity of water, provisions, spare sails, spars, rigging, &c., was attached to a steam tug, and her head turned down stream. As she swung round, the crowd on the wharf gave three cheers. Seventy throats on board responded. Thus we left home.

At six P. M. we passed Pond Island, at the mouth of the river, and half-an-hour later, just outside of Jack Knife Ledge, the tug cast us off, took out the pilot, and returned to the river. There was a moderate breeze from the north-west, but an old sea was heaving in heavily from the south, over the shoal ground. Against this, the ship under her courses, topsails, and topgallant sails, went rearing and plunging seaward.

Heartsick, homesick, and *sea-sick*, I stood upon

the deck and watched the dusky outlines of the coast. The sound of the supper-bell, however, soon interrupted my melancholy observations, and I was requested to go below and assist the steward in waiting upon the tables. I complied, but before I had passed many cups of tea, I received an internal evidence that something was about to occur, for which I should be better prepared on deck, with my head over the rail, than anywhere else, and I left immediately, without apology or explanation, and put my head *there*.

On board a mackerel-catcher, a person engaged as I then was, is said to be "throwing toll," *i. e.* scattering finely-cut bait to attract the fish. The witticisms of fishermen are often more *broad* than deep, but there is, perhaps, analogy enough in this case to base the facetiousness upon.

It is also said that persons thus engaged, are heard to cry from the very depths of their being, "*Europe,*" as if that, forsooth, were the only continent of the old world, or, indeed, of both worlds.

I admit, after reflection, that there is some ground for this report.

And now that I have introduced the subject of sea-sickness, I will muster all my fortitude and go through with it. *All* my fortitude, I say, for when I remember in what a rough-shod manner that detestable disease has ridden over me, first and last, I actually shrink.

A sea-sick man is like a man with the tooth-ache—no, that is not *just* what I mean, for the latter is generally as cross as a starving bear, while the former is very mild and subdued. What I mean *is* that neither gets any sympathy from anybody. Neither, in the popular mind, is it a sickness which is unto death.

This view in regard to sea-sickness, is, however, by many physicians, considered a popular error.

Dr. Barker, of Bellevue Hospital Medical College, New York City, in writing upon the subject, gives three instances of parties known to him, who died from the effects of sea-sickness, and in a very short space of time. And he relates that others have been so prostrated while crossing the Atlantic, that, after landing, weeks elapsed before they were able to go out.

My own experience convinces me that sea-sickness is often injurious to the general health of an individual, though I never knew it to result in death. The popular idea on the subject, however, is that it is never injurious, but often beneficial, and it will be long before that idea is abandoned.

Sea-sickness is one of the ills of life to which all flesh is not heir. Many seamen have never felt any symptoms of it.

Dr. Barker, to whom I have referred, says: "I myself am exempt from the slightest tendency to this affliction, but on the contrary, feel at sea an exhilaration of mind, and an elasticity of body which I do not feel on shore."

And the disease affects differently those suffering from it. Some are violently sick for a short time, and then recover fully. Others never become very sick, but an indescribable nausea pervades them for a long time.

It is the general impression that sea-sickness cannot be prevented, mitigated or cured by medical art.

Dr. Barker is of a different opinion, however. After stating that the *centre* of a vessel, because the motion is less there, is the best place to locate in, he gives the following directions:

1. Have every preparation made at least twenty-four hours before starting, so that the system may not be exhausted by overwork and want of sleep. This direction is particularly important for ladies.

2. Eat as hearty a meal as possible before going on board.

3. Go on board sufficiently early to arrange such things as may be wanted for the first day or two, so that they may be easy of access; then undress and go to bed before the vessel gets under way.

The neglect of this rule, by those who are liable to sea-sickness, is sure to be regretted.

4. Eat regularly and heartily, but without raising the head, for at least one or two days. In this way the habit of digestion is kept up, the strength is preserved, while the system becomes accustomed to the constant change of equilibrium.

5. On the first night out, take some mild laxative pills, as for example, two or three of the compound rhubarb pills.

6. After having become so far habituated to the sea as to be able to take your meals at the table, and to go on deck, never think of rising in the morning until you have eaten something, as a plate of oatmeal porridge, or a cup of coffee or tea, with sea-biscuit or toast.

7. If, subsequently, during the voyage, the sea should become unusually rough, go to bed before getting sick. It is foolish to dare anything when there is no glory to be won, and *something* may be lost.

Such are the Doctor's preventives. I need hardly point out that he can refer only to *passengers*. A *seaman's* lodgings are generally at one *extremity* of the ship, and his sphere of action is bounded horizontally, by the ends of the flying jib and spanker booms, and perpendicularly by the kelson and the main truck. As for *"going to bed,"* he *never* does that. When it is his watch below, he *turns in*. Little allowance is made for sea-sickness before the mast.

But, my young friends, if your horoscopes have been cast, and there are sea voyages before you, just preserve these directions of an experienced physician and practical man, and practice them when you embark, and you may thereby avoid a great deal of genuine suffering.

May avoid mind it, for the Doctor, even, does not promise perfect exemption. And I think even a mitigation doubtful in many cases. It has been proved in some diseases that the medicine that is an antidote for one man, is a bane for another. Indeed, I have been told by an intelligent physician, that there is but one disease, in all the multitude of diseases, for which a specific remedy is known, and that disease is the *itch*.

For the consolation of any of my young readers, who may contemplate " a life on the ocean wave, and a home on the rolling deep," I will say, that, although Dr. Barker has not prescribed for them, or rather they cannot avail themselves of his prescriptions, they will always find those afloat who will be delighted to prescribe for them.

Among these, the disciples of the old school of medicine usually recommend a piece of salt pork with a rope yarn attached, which the patient is required to swallow and draw up again, repeatedly. I once knew a poor simpleton to make use of this remedy. Of course it contributed more to the amusement of the beholders than to the patient's cure.

If the sufferer does not use tobacco, a quid of that delectable stuff is sometimes administered instead of the pork, and the directions in this case are, to chew vigorously and swallow the juice.

The forecastle, however, sometimes contains a Hydropathic practitioner. He, of course, prescribes a cold bath, and this is given by reeving a whip at the end of the fore-yard, one end of which is securely fastened about the patient's ankles, while the other is manned by sympathizing friends. At a given word, he is run up, swung off over the rail, and dropped into the sea. One immersion is usually held to be sufficient for a cure, but sometimes, when the case is an obstinate one, the patient is bowsed up a little way, and dropped a second time.

It is a cruel joke, and not often perpetrated.

There is one phase of sea-sickness that I would not overlook, and which is universally considered dangerous, viz.: when it produces constipation. Ordinary remedies often fail in such instances to move the bowels.

An aggravated case of this kind came to my knowledge, and I will give the remedy which was at length effectual. It is always available on shipboard, and is considered equal to any case. Take half a pint of slush (grease), a pint of salt water, and a pint of molasses, and boil them thoroughly together. A dose—as much as the patient can possibly drink.

The case of which I have a knowledge was this. A brig sailed from New York to Liverpool. The cook was sea-sick—not severely so—but enough to produce constipation of the bowels. The cathartic contents of the medicine chest were exhausted upon him, without effect. Weeks passed on. His sensations were terrible, and the skin of his face grew red, until he was of the complexion of a boiled lobster. A knowledge of the mess I have described above was stowed away among the recollections of the mate. In this emergency it occurred to him. He promptly communicated it to the captain, and offered to prepare it, if he (the captain,) would administer it. He readily promised, and it was prepared. But so disgusting was it, that the sick man vowed he would die before he would swallow it. The captain was equal to the emergency. He presented the tin pot of liquid with one hand, and a rope's end with the other, and gave the cook his choice in these terms: "Take it *now*, or I'll rope's end ye within an inch of your life, and pour it down your throat afterwards."

The cook took it, and it removed the difficulty.

My advice—advice drawn from experience and observation—to any one who ships to do duty on ship-board, and is sea-sick, is, to keep up a *stout heart*, and do as nearly as possible, just what he would do if well. Do you say that you already know that a stout heart is good under all circumstances? Then let me confirm you in that knowledge.

Young friends, when you leave home and relatives to go out into the world, whether the heaving sea lies beneath your feet, or the firm set earth, pray God for a stout heart. Stout to resist loneliness, hardship, pain, scorn, and adversity—and no less stout to meet temptation in its alluring disguises, and the fascinating influences that would lead you from the path of virtue and honor.

But, all this time I have left myself with my head over the rail. Well, it was there quite as long.

After a while, spiritless and stupefied, I crept into my berth. In the darkness my eyes could fix upon no objects, and by degrees my ears failed to catch the dashing of the water and the creaking of the blocks. Gradually I became insensible, and slept a restless, unrefreshing sleep. In the morning I awoke to a day of like miserable existence. And so I endured for a week. Then the end came. Oh, it was a long and cruel initiation!

I came out of it weak, thin, and pale. With

hard salt beef and flinty sea-biscuits I lined my unsteady ribs. Never did the daintiest food taste so well. My long abstinence had ground my appetite, and the healthy, bracing air of the sea whetted it to a perfect edge.

They only who have been sea-sick, can properly appreciate sea-sickness. It cannot be perfectly described. It is not, in the general sense of the term, anguish, but it takes away the strength and manliness of a man.

A sense of nausea pervades him. He lies down. Action is the most obnoxious of things to him. He would hardly struggle to save his life.

When I had regained strength and animation, and had slept sweetly and soundly, I looked around me and beheld a new existence.

A blue sky, flecked with a few clouds, came down and met the sea. Against it blue waves leaped joyously out of the bosom of the blue sea. The great bright sun shone down. The wind swept cheerily by, and the ship, seemingly free and joyous, like all around her, drove swiftly along the waves.

How my heart was lifted up and expanded! What a sense of freedom and joy pervaded my whole being. I felt an impulse to clap my hands and leap like the waves.

There was no sense of loneliness, though, save a consciousness of the presence of God, we were solitary and alone. He—who is both the mythical Jove and the mythical Neptune—can fill space with His presence, and people it with images of His power and glory. He is a cord connecting in the mind the past, the present, and all time to come. On Him the trusting heart leans daily, and to Him the eye of faith is constantly directed. If we go back to our cradles and our mother's arms, all the past speaks of Him—and if we tell our hopes of the future, we humbly add, "Providence permitting."

We would not for worlds lose this consciousness of His presence—we could not if we would.

"Whither shall I go from thy Spirit, or whither shall I flee from thy presence?

"If I ascend up into heaven, thou art there; if I make my bed in hell, behold thou art there.

"If I take the wings of the morning and dwell in *the uttermost parts of the sea, even there* shall thy hand lead me, and thy right hand shall hold me."

My dear reader, if you have an Atlas convenient, just take it, please, and open to the map of North America. Near the north-eastern extremity of the United States, you will be likely to see a delineation, longer or shorter, of the River Kenebec. Place the end of your pencil upon the mouth of the river, and then move it in a south-easterly direction, until you reach the straight line running across the map that indicates the fortieth parallel of north latitude. Is there anything peculiarly interesting in this locality?

CHAPTER III.

THE GULF STREAM.

HOW was the question at the end of the last chapter answered? The locality I designated is decidedly an interesting one. It is in the midst of the *Gulf Stream*. And what is that? It is a rapid river in the ocean, with banks of water, and a bed of water, and yet none the less emphatically a *river*. We can describe it just as any other river. It rises in the Gulf of Mexico, runs in a northeasterly direction with a constantly widening channel and decreasing velocity, until, from a vast mouth, spanning almost the western coast of Europe, it empties northerly into the Arctic Ocean, to the east of Greenland, and southerly into the Bay of Biscay, reaching even, as a distinctive current, the Azores and Canaries.

What *makes* this Gulf Stream, or river, do you ask? Ah, who shall tell? He knows who "answered Job out of the whirlwind, and said * * * Hast thou entered into the springs of the sea? or hast thou walked in the search of the depth?" And He alone *knows.*

But there are many *theories* about it. Each theory probably satisfied its author and his admirers, but not the authors of other theories, or their admirers.

It was in this majestic oceanic river that we found ourselves after a few days' sail from Bath. Its waters were of a deep and glorious blue, which is a characteristic of this stream, particularly near its source. And another characteristic was also quite perceptible—a shorter and sharper sea. My interest in anything was not excessive at this time, on account of causes detailed in the preceeding chapter. But despite all untoward circumstances, the scene impressed me deeply, having been all my life accustomed to green water and a circumscribed horizon.

The Gulf Stream I have said originates in the Gulf of Mexico. Cast your eyes again upon the map. Between the Peninsula of Florida and the Bahama group of the West India Islands, you behold a narrow channel of clear water. Up this the Gulf Stream pours impetuously. Its width here is thirty-two miles, its depth three hundred and seventy fathoms, and its velocity between four and five miles per hour. And here its color is of an intense indigo blue. Its limits, or borders, are so distinct, on this account, that on sailing into it, one can readily tell when the vessel enters it, when she is half way into it, and when she is quite into it.

Off Cape Hatteras, in North Carolina, its width is seventy-five miles, and its velocity three miles per hour. Off the Grand Banks, away up to Newfoundland, its course becomes more easterly than formerly, but there has been all along, the same widening of its channel, and diminishing of its velocity, that was observable before.

Besides its current and its color, the Gulf Stream possesses another peculiarity of more consequence than these. Its waters are very warm—possess a very high temperature. In the channel between Florida and the Bahamas, its temperature is nine degrees higher than that of the water that forms its banks. When it reaches the Grand Banks it is still six degrees warmer.

Dr. Franklin, who was first to discover the tractability of lightening, and also the first to enunciate the great truth, that "God governs in the affairs of nations," was first to call public attention to this wonderful phenomena.

It happened in this wise: When Franklin was in London, in 1770, he was consulted in regard to a memorial which the Board of Customs at Boston, had sent to the Lords of the Treasury, stating that the King's packets from Falmouth were generally two weeks longer making the passage from Falmouth to Boston, than were the common traders in going from London to Providence, R. I. They therefore asked that the Falmouth packets be sent to Providence instead of Boston.

As the distance was not a little less between Falmouth and Boston than between London and Providence, the Doctor was surprised; but he was unwilling to admit, without some investigation, "that the longest way round was the shortest way home." In pushing his inquiries, he consulted Capt. Folger, a Nantucket whaler, who was also in London at this time.

The Captain readily explained that the difference in the passage arose from · this fact. The Rhode Island captains were acquainted with the Gulf Stream, and kept out of it, while the captains of the King's packets, knowing nothing about it, kept in it, and were set back about fifty miles a day. Capt. Folger had become acquainted with it while in the pursuit of whales. These animals (what say, boys, is a whale an *animal* or a *fish*, or both, or neither?) were found on both sides of the warm current, but never in it.

Of course, the Doctor, having found a clue, made a determined effort to follow it up, and penetrate, if possible, the penetralia of nature.

His theory of the production of the Gulf Stream

I will give by and by. Of the remainder of his labors it is sufficient to say here, that he called public attention pretty thoroughly to the facts he had learned. And public attention has never ceased to be given to this interesting subject.

Having had their attention called to it so long, have men discovered any utility, any beneficent purpose, in this Gulf Stream?

This fact has become apparent. If there were not some agent to carry off much of the heat generated in that great basin of which the Gulf of Mexico is the bottom, it would be so great as to make this region the hottest, and most pestilential in the world. The Gulf Stream *is* such an agent, and surely here is beneficence and utility as well.

Having blessed the dwellers at its source, has it any blessings for those who dwell at its mouth?

Open the Atlas again. Our latitude is about 42° North. Turn to the map of Europe and find the parallel there. You see it crosses Northern Spain and the South of France. Will our climate compare in mildness with the climate of those countries? No, truly. Why? Wait a moment.

Great Britain and Ireland may be said to lie in the fifty-third degree of north latitude, as that parallel crosses nearly in the centre of each. Now, how does our climate compare with that of Great Britain and Ireland, eleven degrees farther north?

It is colder. To what shall we attribute this remarkable difference? To the Gulf Stream, *for we know that it is the cause.* The west wind, which is the prevailing one, blowing across its surface, bears its warm exhalations over these lands; and against the shores of these lands its warm current is also impelled. Its influence does not end here, but may be traced along the west coast of Norway, and far up where Spitzbergen lies, at the threshold of perpetual ice.

How wonderful! These lands warmed in winter by a furnace placed in the Gulf of Mexico, and the heat sent through a pipe thousands of miles long. But for this provision of nature, Great Britain would be as bleak, as inhospitable, and as uninhabitable as Labrador, to which it corresponds in latitude.

But are the benefits of the Gulf Stream confined to its extremities? No. Vessels bound to New York, and ports of New England, in winter, meet with severe cold, and terrible gales off the coast. And when hugging the frosty hurricanes, off these ports of destination, they become unmanageable, from the ice that accumulates in masses on everything, is it not a benefit to have these warm waters right under the lee? In this place of refuge the ice will quickly disappear, and chilled and stiffened fingers grow warm and limber again. There is summer heat in the Gulf Stream in the dead of winter.

There the weather worn mariner may refit his vessel, and recruit his energies for another trial.

Do vessels take advantage of this provision of Providence? As a matter of course. Without the Gulf Stream the coast would not be navigable in winter.

Two years ago I conversed with a ship-master who had just arrived in Boston from New Orleans. Four times, he said, he was inside of Cape Cod, and each time encountered weather that compelled him to put his helm up, and with his ship's waist full of ice, and every rope as big as his leg, run back into the Gulf Stream and thaw out. He said it was a great relief to him when he got into port, a statement to which, after what he had told me, I was prepared to give full credit.

In other respects the Gulf Stream benefits the mariner. Its presence indicates to him that he has approached the coast; and by keeping in it when bound to the eastward, he can make greater progress.

And now we will view this accommodating stream in another character—one in which it accomplishes results that are at the same time very beneficial to the mariner, and very interesting to all classes of society.

You know that King Cold, from his extensive dock-yards, away up north, is constantly dispatching his armadas of icebergs down to the portions of the Atlantic sacred to commerce.

Men could not contend with these, and could they pass the limits to which they are now confined, they would sweep the seas of warlike and peaceful navies alike.

Now who has confined them to certain limits? Who comes to the rescue of the race here? It is King Heat, the eternal enemy of King Cold, with whom he has warred, with varying success, since the beginning of time. From his throne in the Gulf of Mexico, he saw the peril of man, and poured the warm waters of the Gulf Stream up the coast. They meet the cold currents of the North, and the ice squadrons of King Cold, off Newfoundland, and there has been the battle-field.

Do you ask me where are the wrecks of battle that strew this mighty field? Behold them—*the Grand Banks of Newfoundland!*

The Grand Banks are the deposits of the Gulf Stream, and the icebergs jointly. The former, on account of the chilly currents from the north, deposits here the infusoria and corpses of living things brought forth in its warm waters. The latter, melted by the warm current from the south, deposit here their loads of stone and earth, torn off from the Arctic continent.

It is wonderful!

Now if all these facts impress you as they ought, you will ask if there are the same evidences of the Creator's wisdom here, that are observable in His other works.

There is this fact about the Gulf Stream that is very striking and beautiful. One of its offices is to convey heat from the Gulf region to the cold regions of the north. Earth is a good conductor of heat, and did this stream in any part of its course touch the crust of the earth, much of the heat would be conducted off. But it nowhere does. Though flowing near the land on one side, and near the bottom of the sea in one part of its course, it is everywhere protected from contact by cushions of cold water, an excellent *non-conductor* of heat.

Now a few words concerning the theories by which the flow of the Gulf Stream is accounted for. One has been fairly demolished, and I will refer to that first. It was that the Mississippi River produced the Gulf Stream. The two following facts overthrew this theory.

1. The Gulf Stream discharges from the Gulf of Mexico three thousand times as much water as the Mississippi pours into it.

2. The Mississippi is *fresh*, while the Gulf Stream is *excessively salt*.

There are other theories which cannot be said to be fairly demolished. It is held by some now, and was held by many once, that the daily motion of the earth on its axis, causes a rotary motion of the waters upon it from east to west. Every boy who has turned a grindstone that had water poured upon it, knows how this is. The shape of the South American coast forced vast volumes of this moving water into the Gulf of Mexico between that continent and Cuba. The issue of this water, in a contrary direction, is the Gulf Stream.

Dr. Franklin, however, and many other scientific men with him, held that the Gulf Stream is the escape, from the Gulf of Mexico, of water forced into it by the *trade winds*. Of these trade winds I shall have occasion to speak hereafter. The two theories agree upon a head of water in the Gulf as the cause of the stream, but do not agree as to how that head of water came there.

Lieut. Maury lays down this theorem—" The dynamical force (that is, the force of *water in motion*) that calls forth the Gulf Stream, is found in the difference, as to specific gravity, of intertropical and polar waters."

Do you understand this? If I do, it means this: The extremes of polar cold, and equatorial heat, so act upon the waters subject to their influence as to disturb their equibibrium. It is a law of water, that when its equilibrium is disturbed, it will not rest until it is restored. Now here are two agents continually disturbing the equilibrium of the great body of water on the globe, and an inexorable war as constantly compelling a restoration of that equilibrium. What is the result? Oceanic currents, of course, and one of them, Maury says, is the Gulf Stream.

It is a great subject, worthy of study, and repaying study. It will stand any amount of discussion, and it receives any amount of it.

CHAPTER IV.

CONCERNING THE SHIP, HER CREW, AND SOMETHING CONCERNING SEA USAGES.

AT the time of which I write, a ship of five hundred tons belonged rather to the largest class of ships than to the smallest. Seven hundred tons for a merchant ship, was quite large, one thousand tons monstrous, and a ship of twelve hundred tons seemed a perfect leviathan.

At the present time a ship of seven hundred tons is small, one of two thousand tons not extremely large, and very many reach a number above three thousand.

The gigantic, not only in living creatures, but also in things, compels our admiration. We may, indeed, pay the same amount of money to see Tom Thumb that we would pay to see the Belgian Giant, but then the admission fee don't determine our impressions at all. There is no object—seamen think so at all events, and always will—that more deeply impresses a beholder than one of these monster, modern ships, fully rigged, whether under sail, or with canvass furled. To a landsman the maze of rigging is perfectly bewildering—a labyrinth to which he can discover no clue.

A friend once told me that he was one day standing on a wharf in Baltimore, at the end of which lay a very large ship, discharging a cargo of guano, which she had brought from the Chincha Islands. While there he observed a man, evidently a countryman, come slowly down the wharf, looking carelessly to right and left. He was quite near the ship before his eyes seemed to rest fairly upon her.

Then he approached still nearer, and looked slowly from end to end of the vast hull, his eyes examining curiously the enormous channels of the ship.

And then he glanced upward, and as he did so, an expression of intense amazement crept into his countenance.

Suddenly dropping his eyes until they rested upon the lower yard of the main-mast, he counted loudly and impressively, "*one.*" Tipping back his head until it formed a right angle with his spinal column, he continued counting, as his eyes rested successively upon the lower topsail, upper topsail, topgallant, royal, and skysail yards, "*Two—Three—Four—Five—Six.*" Then, without a change of position, he raised both hands towards heaven, and exclaimed, "*Good Lord!*"

But all this is irrelevant. My intention is to describe to you our ship and ship's company.

The Hampton was double decked, and had also a poop deck. A poop deck is a part of a deck, extending from the stern of a ship, to a greater or less distance, towards the bow. The poop deck of the Hampton extended forward to a point just beyond the mainmast. So there was a projection of this deck beyond the bulkhead, of about six feet.

In the open space beneath, the pumps were located. There were also openings on each side of this projection, through which flights of steps led from the main deck up to the poop. The space under the poop deck was divided into two parts by a partition thwart ships, just forward of the mizzenmast. The after part was finished into a cabin, and made a very comfortable, commodious and pretty one. It was lighted by skylights in the deck above, and windows in the stern. The captain's stateroom is usually the aftermost one on the starboard side, which is the right hand side, looking forward. On board the Hampton the captain's room was quite large, containing, besides an ample berth, a chest of drawers, a book case, chart box, chronometer case, &c. It was lighted by a window in the stern. A raised seat, called the transom locker, extended across the whole cabin. This was furnished with stuffed cushions, and was a very comfortable place to sit down, or lie down.

Opposite the captain's state room, was the water closet. The cabin contained six state rooms, besides these. There were two entrances, one by a gangway and steps, from the deck above, and the other from the main deck forward.

The remaining space under the poop deck, forward of the cabin, was, at this time, fitted up with berths, and occupied by passengers. It was denominated the *forward* cabin, while the other was known as the *after* cabin.

On the main deck, just forward of the main hatch, and extending nearly to the foremast, was a house. This house was divided into three parts. The after and larger part was designed to accommodate the ship's crew. Next was the galley, where the cook reigned over the pots and kettles. The forward part was a store room. The crew, however, instead of being lodged in the house designed for them, were, at this time, in a forecastle, temporarily fitted up in "the eyes of the ship," between decks, where such institutions usually are.

The house I have described was occupied by several passengers, the second and third mates, the carpenter, my brother and myself.

There need not be much said about the spars,

and rigging, or sails. While ships differ very much in their arrangements upon deck, they differ very little aloft, save that some carry a greater number of sails than others. If you are acquainted with the sails and rigging on board of one ship, you will find that knowledge quite available on board of any other.

The ship's company, exclusive of passengers, numbered twenty-four, consisting of four officers, (captain and three mates,) two stewards, one cook, fourteen seamen, and three boys, the latter count including myself, who was rated as cabin boy.

This was an unusually large crew for a ship of the Hampton's size, but, with a few exceptions, all were working their way. It was the easiest thing in the world, then, to ship a crew to go to San Francisco, but, as we afterwards experienced, the most difficult to ship one to sail from it.

When a ship leaves port there is generally plenty of work for all hands. The anchors are to be secured, chains unbent and stowed away, everything moveable chocked and lashed, decks cleared up, &c. At night the watches are chosen. On board of merchant ships the men are divided into two watches. On men-of-war, where men are more plentiful, and owners richer, there are three watches.

While I was gazing from the poop, with a woe-begone expression, at the shores of Maine, fast receding in the distance and the darkness, the operation of choosing watches was going on, on the main deck. The mates had proceeded thither, and summoned the men before them. The mate then selected a man, who responded to the call by going over to the port side. Next the second mate chose, and his man responded by passing over to the starboard side. This was continued until all were chosen, including the man at the wheel, who went to starboard or port, in count only, of course.

Any inequalities in watches thus chosen—and the men being generally unknown to the officers, there must occasionally be such—are adjusted when they become apparent.

The exempts from standing watch, are the cook, steward, and cabin boy. The captain is also an exempt, but it must not be inferred from this that he sleeps all night always. Great responsibility rests upon him, and in bad weather he is below but little, night or day.

A "trick" at the wheel is two hours in length. The space of time that one keeps a lookout at night is also two hours. The order in which these "tricks" and lookouts shall occur, is settled by the mate. The man on lookout, except in very bad weather, is stationed on the topgallant forecastle, a short deck in the bows of a ship, about four or five feet above the main deck. This is a very bleak and wet place, and in bad weather, the lookout (meaning the man,) is allowed a lee, if he can find a convenient one.

In front of the man at the wheel is the binnacle, a place for the ship's compasses. There is placed in this, at night, a lamp which illuminates the compasses. In it, also, a time-piece is placed, and on it, within reach of the steersman's hand, is a small stationary bell, with a short lanyard or string, tied to the tongue. On the topgallant forecastle is a much larger bell, arranged in the same way.

We will suppose now, if you please, that it is midnight on board the ship. The larboard watch has just gone below, and the starboard watch has the deck.

The second mate, who has charge, paces the poop, his eyes roving in all directions, up at the sails, forward into the gloom that is there, astern into the gloom that is there, always restless and observant. Anon he approaches the wheel and gazes into the binnacle. There the helmsman stands, grasping the spokes of the wheel, and his eyes watch incessantly the compass, the sails, and the stars. Perched on the forecastle, the lookout sweeps all before with constant glances. *Clang!* It is half past twelve, and the helmsman has struck "one bell." The lookout seizes the lanyard attached to the tongue of the larger bell at his side, and in a heavier tone responds " one bell."

At one o'clock "two bells" are struck aft, and repeated forward. "Three bells" announce half past one, and "four bells" two o'clock. As the lookout responds to "four bells," the word goes round to "relieve the wheel," which is a figure of speech meaning relieve *the man at the wheel*. Immediately (if he be a considerate man,) the next on the schedule proceeds aft.

There is a great deal of etiquette observed on ship board, and if the ship is sailing with the wind on one side, the men go to, and return from the wheel on the opposite, or lee side. When the ship is running dead before the wind, with square yards, the starboard is, by general usage, the weather side, and is respected as such by seamen. When the relief reaches the wheel, and places his hands upon the spokes released by the other, he pricks up his ears so as to hear correctly the course. "South-south-east," says the relieved man. "South-south-east," repeats the relief, and the wheel is relieved. Pronounce the above named course as if spelled *sow'-suth-east*, if you wish to be nautical.

At half past two the new man at the wheel strikes "five bells," and the new lookout responds accordingly. *Sometimes* there is no response, because, from thinking of his sweetheart, or because he is a numbhead, anyway, the look-out has gone to sleep. The watchful officer listens for the response. Often the man's watchmates make it for him, or wake him, and it is done tardily. But sometimes they neither wake him, nor do it for him. Then the officer, muttering wrathfully, descends to the main deck, draws a bucket of water, and steals forward. *Slap-dash!* It is all over the poor fellow, and his returning senses are greeted by a hearty kick, and, "Calking are ye, you lubber, you horse-marine, you owl of the woods! Take that," repeating the kick, "and keep your eyelids pinned back in *my* watch, my son."

The officer goes back to his station molified, and when "six bells" are struck aft, denoting three o'clock, there is sure to be a prompt response from the forecastle.

At half past three, "seven bells" are struck, and at four, "eight bells."

The look-out follows the last stroke of "eight bells" by, "*and call the watch.*" Whereupon a sailor takes a handspike, and thunders for a few moments on the deck, and then, putting his head into the entrance of the forecastle, he *intones* the required formula—"Larboard watch, a h-o-y! Eight bells! Wake up sleepers, and *turn out!*"

The sleepers wake up, and turn out, and make their toilets by the light of a tin lamp, filled with slush, and having a rope yarn for a wick. Meanwhile the second mate has, in a less boisterous way, called his brother officer, and in a few moments the watches are changed, and all is quiet save the regularly recurring strokes of the bell, which, beginning at "one bell," check off the lapsing half hours.

At "seven bells" in the morning watch, that is at half past seven o'clock, all hands are called to breakfast. Before this, the watch on duty have washed the decks, a thing that is done every morning under all circumstances. As it is far from the rail of a ship to the water, and it would be very laborious to draw all the water for washing decks from the sea in buckets, a pump is generally placed in some part of a ship to raise the water for this purpose. On board the Hampton this pump was forward, just by the bowsprit. The water came up in a copper pipe, set into the stem. The pumper stood on the forecastle (short for *topgallant* forecastle). The water ran through a pipe under the forecastle deck, into a large tub on the main deck. From this it was dipped in buckets and passed about the deck. The deck is wet, scrubbed and rinsed.

As water is always plentiful, enough is used on each occasion to put out a moderate conflagration. After the washing was done the poop deck was usually swabbed dry.

It will be readily seen that dividing the twenty-four hours into six watches of four hours each, would bring one watch on deck at the same hours each night—*i. e.* of the twelve hours pertaining to the night, one watch would constantly be on deck eight hours, and the other but four. To change this order, the watch from four P. M. to eight P. M. is divided into two, called "dog watches." At five the decks are swept cleanly, and at six supper is eaten. From six to eight, the last dog watch, all hands are generally on deck, and generally at leisure. This is the time, in pleasant weather, for sky-larking, for yarning, for smoking, and for singing.

Some one may ask why these short watches are called *dog* watches.

I have heard two explanations of a humorous character.

One is that the term is a corruption of *dock* watch—a full watch *docked*, or cut down; the other is that it is a *cur*-tailing of a full watch, and is, therefore, properly termed a *dog* watch.

Seamen make puns and deliver themselves of a great deal of very fair humorous matter.

A ship is called *she* contrary to the spirit of grammatical usage. I have heard this reason for it given: "A ship is of the feminine gender, because, like a woman, her rigging costs more than her hull."

Amusing, if you never saw it before, but it's old and threadbare, and besides, it's abominable and slanderous, and excessively unjust to the women, whom may God bless continually.

CHAPTER V.

A BURIAL AT SEA.—SEAMEN'S SUPERSTITIONS.

WHEN twenty days out, a passenger, Ezra Whitman, of Waterville, Me., died. He had been ill from the outset of the voyage. Day after day he grew feebler, and on the twenty-ninth of September, expired.

He had set out with us upon a long voyage— to sail over the Atlantic and Pacific waters. But, thus early on our way, he left us and embarked, *alone*, upon a far longer voyage, and upon an ocean vaster than the added Atlantic and Pacific, the great Ocean of Eternity, which lies beyond the duration of Time.

But he went not as an adventurer or discoverer, without direction or destination. He committed his frail bark to Christ, the faithful Pilot, and steered for that city whose twelve gates are twelve pearls, and whose streets are of pure gold. Oh, happy destination!

Betimes, we reached our port, and entered its "Golden Gate," and trod its thronged streets. We saw its god, King Mammon, and his multitudinous worshippers flocking from the corners of the earth. But happier he who had entered the city with the gates of pearl. Fire, and all manner of desolation, has scathed the "City of the Golden Gate," and its inhabitants go from it and return no more. But in the city with the gates of pearl "there shall be no more curse; but the throne of God and the Lamb shall be in it; and his servants shall serve him. * * * And there shall be no night there; and they shall need no candle, neither light of the sun; for the Lord God giveth them light, and they shall reign forever and ever."

It was afternoon when poor Whitman's body was committed to the deep. There was no wind—not a breath. Since morning not a catspaw had wandered by; but the sea, blue as the sky, stretched far away, smooth, glassy and unbroken. The flag was set half mast. It hung straight down in vertical folds, opening and shutting slightly with the monotonous motion of the ship, as she fell and rose, slowly, on the long ocean swell.

At two o'clock the body of the deceased, sewed up in canvass, and with heavy weights at the feet, was borne out of the cabin. A plank, laid in the starboard gangway, received it. The feet were placed outboard. The whole ship's company, with uncovered heads, assembled around. Almost perfect silence ensued. There was no sound of animate thing, save the twitter of the stormy-petrel—no sound of inanimate thing, only the bellying and collapsing sails. The service (that of the Church of England,) was read by one of the passengers. The reading was audible to all, though sad and low.

"Man that is born of woman, hath but a short time to live, and is full of misery. He cometh up, and is cut down like a flower; he fleeth as it were a shadow, and never continueth in one stay.

"In the midst of life we are in death. Of whom may we seek for succor, but of Thee, O Lord, who for our sins art justly displeased?

"Yet, O Lord God most holy, O Lord most mighty, O holy and most merciful Savior, deliver us not into the bitter pains of eternal death.

"Thou knowest, Lord, the secrets of our hearts. Shut not thy merciful ears to our prayers; but spare us, Lord most holy, O God most mighty, O holy and merciful Savior, thou most worthy Judge Eternal, suffer us not, at our last hour, for any pains of death, to fall from thee.

"Forasmuch as it hath pleased Almighty God, in His wise providence, to take out of this world the soul of our deceased brother, we therefore commit his body to the deep, to be turned into corruption, looking to the resurrection of the body, when the sea shall give up her dead, and the life of the world to come, through our Lord Jesus Christ; who at his coming shall change our vile body, according to the mighty working whereby he is able to subdue all things to himself."

When the words " we therefore commit his body to the deep," were pronounced, the end of the plank which supported the head of the corpse was raised, and the body slid with a gentle motion from it, and fell heavily into the water. From my position I could look over the side. I did look. Under the gangway the ripple in the water was widening, and the bubbles breaking, and down many feet under the surface was the body, in its white cerements, gliding obliquely away.

Poor brother! Above thy resting place no green grass grows—no fair flowers bloom. And only the winged bird, the winged ship, and the invisible wind, can tread the surface o'er thy head.

The services were ended. Thoughtful and silent, but relieved, the seamen turned away. A corpse on board a ship is a weight upon the hearts of all her mariners. Their tones are subdued, and their words and thoughts take a melancholy turn. They cannot forget the fact. There is a constant and oppressive anticipation of evil in their minds. Look they up to heaven, or down into the deep, or abroad upon the waste of waters, it is to behold some coming evil, some strange, supernatural, overpowering woe.

It is one of the seaman's peculiar superstitions. He is a strange being. He fears not the wind, or the sea, the whizzing cannon ball, or the levelled pike. These are of earth. He knows them, and in conflict dares defy them. But when God's mysterious hand hath been laid upon a shipmate, and hath set free from the body the imprisoned spirit, then the seaman feels a power upon him that he cannot resist. For there is on him no armor of scientific truth to ward off his thick coming and mysterious thoughts. May not the freed spirit (he reasons about it thus,) visit its old abode of clay? In what guise will it come, if come it does? Will I behold it? And if so, can I, unscathed, front a tenant of unearthly worlds?

They do, indeed, have strange fancies. One calm day upon the passage I got a billet of wood, and went aft to hurl it at the flocks of Mother Cary's Chickens, hovering about the stern. As I stood with my arm raised, waiting for a good opportunity, the man at the wheel observed me.

"What are you about?" he asked me suddenly.

"I am going to heave this at the birds," I answered.

With one nervous hand the great, big whiskered, and bronzed man steadied the jerking wheel, and the other extended towards me.

"Boy,"—he was in earnest I knew by the depth of his voice—"Boy, do you wish to see your home again?"

I knew his meaning and attempted a laugh. I was too much awed by his manner, however, to succeed. He went on—

"Kill one of them, and you'll see but few more suns rise, mind you that. This ship will sink, and every soul on board her, if you draw a drop of blood, or knock a feather from such birds as you see there."

"Why?" I questioned, though I foresaw his reply.

"*They're sailors' souls.* Think of your friends, my lad, and if you love them drop that stick."

I dared not, in the presence of that earnest man, and with his prophetic words ringing in my ears, use my missile. I dropped it from my hand, which had grown strangely nerveless. It fell overboard, and when the ship, pounding the water with her counter, had impelled it a few feet from her, the birds it was designed to destroy gathered noisily about it.

Subsequently, Dr. Burleigh, the dispenser of pills and emetics, brought up his rifle to practice firing.

After breaking a bottle, suspended from the end of the mainyard by a ropeyarn, and shooting the yarn off in the middle, he announced his intention of killing a Mother Carey's Chicken in full flight on the wing. There was a general conviction that he would do it the first time firing, and the interest was great. The Doctor charged his rifle carefully, bent the cock, and raised the butt to his shoulder.

At the same moment two stout hands were laid upon the barrel, one stout hand upon each of his shoulders, and a very earnest voice said in his ear:

"Doctor, don't fire."

Two sailors, who had been occupied in the vicinity, had taken the matter up.

The Doctor was furious, and swore he *would* shoot, and shoot *them*, if they did not desist. They struggled together, and no one offered to interfere.

"Here, Captain," the Doctor shouted, finding them resolute, "come here."

The captain approached from the other end of the poop deck. Before he reached them he divined the cause of the difficulty.

"Men," said he, "go back to your work. Doctor"—but I will not endeavor to repeat his words. Let it suffice to say that he convinced the Doctor of an important fact, viz., that to secure cheerful obedience, alacrity, and a wholesome humor in a ship's company, one must respect their peculiar convictions, where such convictions cannot possibly interfere with the goods, the rights, or the property of others, or violate any principle or practice of decent men.

So, good was wrought by superstition in both these cases. I killed no birds and the Doctor killed none. Shame on us both that we thought to do so.

And shame on you, my young readers, if ever wantonly, and for sport, you take the life of any harmless, living thing. Not that any such are the souls of dead men, for that is a monstrous superstition; but God gave them their lives, which no human art can restore when lost. What *right* to kill them can you claim? They, too, are under our Heavenly Father's supervision. Not one of them falls to the ground without His knowledge, Christ has said, and though *you* may forget the murder of one in a day, He will remember it all the days of time, and His spirit will convict you of it when it will seem very heinous in your eyes.

I will now enumerate briefly some other things that excite the sailor's superstition.

The sailing of a ship on *Friday* is widely known as a cause of uneasiness to her mariners. They term it "the unlucky day," and the stoutest hearted old sea dog among them has dismal forebodings whenever the subject is discussed.

In order to correct this superstition, a wealthy merchant once laid the keel of a ship on Friday, launched her on Friday, named her "Friday," and sent her to sea on Friday.

Singularly enough, she was never heard of again,

and, instead of correcting the superstition, this whole affair seemed to confirm it absolutely.

On the other hand, my father, a ship master of fifty years standing, always sailed on Friday, if possible, and few men, I think, have made so many voyages and met with so few accidents.

Should a shark persist in following a ship for any length of time, it would be regarded as an omen of ill. Say the sailors, "He is after a meal of man's flesh."

And they are confident that a wonderful instinct has assured the voracious creature that he will get it—confident that some one will fall overboard into his jaws, or die and be committed to the sea. They can cite a thousand instances where this has happened in their own, and others' experience.

The perching of atmospheric meteors upon the spars is a prognostication of disaster. They are *evil eyes*, say they, and whatsoever ship they look upon is destined to shipwreck and ruin, unless saved by the special good guardianship of God.

Continued calms, or continued storms, revive the story of the disobedient prophet, voyaging from Joppa to Tarshish. There is a mental casting of lots, and he upon whom the lot falls, might well exclaim with the ancient mariner—

> "Ah! well-a-day, what evil looks
> *Have* I from old and young."

He is not cast overboard, like Jonah of old, but he is distrusted on all sides, and becomes an alien from the little commonwealth.

However, with the extension of commerce, and a greater amount of education, these old superstitions are dying out.

There is something fascinating to the mind, even to the most polished mind, in such things. We all have a leaning in our natures toward the marvelous and supernatural. But it would be a happy thing if seamen would exchange their peculiar notions for a belief in a kind and ever watchful Providence.

There are no malignant stars. Every motion in the sea and air begins with God, and every pulse-beat in every creature of the sea and air. The "stirrer of the storm" is subject to his will. He works in all, and through all, not for the harm of any, but for the good of all.

The superstition of the ancient mariners is gone with all its train of imaginary horrors. Scylla and Charybdis do not terrify now. The Sirens' songs have ceased, and Circe's fatal cup was shattered long ago. But the heavens are still the same. Castor and Pollux shine as benignly now as when Horace committed to their care the ship of Virgil. And *all* the stars look down unchanged and steadfast. The sun and moon do rise and set the same. And thus, ever, regardless of the ebb and flow of man's imagination, will God's good gifts abide.

CHAPTER VI.

THE SARGASSO SEA.

I THINK I have said that I was cabin boy. In a little time it became apparent, even to me, that I was not giving perfect satisfaction to those who were most interested in my labors. You see, I had great curiosity to know all that was going on—and, by the way, you show me a boy that does not have great curiosity, and I will show you a greater wonder than ever Barnum exhibited. The result of this great curiosity with me was that, when a strange sail was announced, I immediately left my work and began the ascent of the main rigging, not pausing until I could throw a leg over the main topsail yard, and there I remained a fixture as long as anything was likely " to turn up."

A day or two after the burial of Whitman, described in the preceeding chapter, I was plying my avocation (scouring knives and forks) in the pantry. The pantry was under the poop deck, just by one of the entrances to the cabin.

I was not so deeply interested in my business as not to be aware suddenly of an unusual stir on both decks. I threw my Bristol brick and cork in one direction, and my knives and forks in another, and hurried out. It was a beautiful day. The wind was moderate from the north-east, just aft the beam, and the sea smooth as a mill pond. There was evidently much interest excited among all on deck, for some were going aloft, and many standing on the rail; and from the direction in which all eyes were turned, and all hands pointing, the interesting object, whatever it might be, lay to the south-east.

I leaped into the rigging, and lost no time in making my way to my accustomed perch on the maintopsail yard. It was already occupied, but I thrust myself forward, and looking off on the larboard bow, saw, a mile or thereabouts away, what, at first glance, seemed a low, level island. A moment's observation, however, served to dispel this illusion.

Its surface conformed to the surface of the waves, rising and falling with them. It must then be a vast field of floating material. Of what could it be composed? In regard to this, one could not long remain in uncertainty who made a good use of his senses. All about the ship could be seen small patches of floating sea-weed.

The great mass was certainly of the same matter, but on what a gigantic scale! The patches were small islets; this was a great continent.

After taking a good long look, I descended to the deck, and edged up to a group of after-cabin passengers who were learnedly discussing the phenomena.

One made a remark something like this: "These great fields don't seem to constantly occupy one locality. East India ship-masters report falling in with them on different meridians."

Another man immediately said: "The Government ought to have instructed Com. Wilkes to make a thorough investigation of the sea hereabouts. He could have settled a good many of these vexed questions."

"Then, after all," I said to myself, "it's nothing new."

New! Go back with me over the eighteen Christian centuries, and the three pagan centuries that immediately preceeded the birth of Christ. At that remote time, we are told, a ship of Gades (now Cadiz, in Spain), while sailing along the coast, was driven by a furious north-east wind far out into the great unknown ocean, towards the setting sun —driven, until at length they found themselves entangled among vast and intertwined masses of floating sea-weed.

Here the wind had no power to drive them farther, and when it abated and changed, they hastened to extricate their ship, and hurried away from this strange region in terror and dismay.

In 1492, as we have all been taught, Columbus, embarking at Palos, sailed into this same unknown sea, and encountered the same floating fields of weed, and his crew expressed the same terror and dismay. And from that day to this, ships have navigated that sea, and the wonderful spectacle has not failed to greet the mariner's eyes on each occasion.

At length, the Spaniards and Portugese, who navigated it the most, named it the *Mar de Sargasso*, the Weedy Sea.

I think I hear some inquisitive reader ask, "How does all that sea-weed get there?" Oh yes, how does it get there! Some things are hard to tell, and this is one.

But, luckily, we have learned men among us, who stick at nothing, and who will furnish you with a reason for anything that exists, for *all* that exists, and for much that don't exist.

These learned men have a theory to account for the existence of the Sargasso Sea, and I, for one, believe in it.

It is easy to illustrate this theory. Fill a pail with water, throw in some bits of wood, and whirl it around rapidly in one direction. Set it down and observe it. The water is moving rapidly around in it—most rapidly near the edges, but in the centre it is almost still. Where are the bits of wood? In the still water in the centre.

Now let us see if we can find any analogy between our pail and the Central Atlantic.

Open your Atlas and find the map containing this region. I told you in a former chapter, that the Gulf Stream, which issues from the Gulf of Mexico, could be traced, *via* Cape Hatteras and the Grand Banks, to the Canaries. It does not stop there, but flows on south, past the Cape de Verde Islands, until it strikes and joins the great Equatorial current, which, issuing from the Gulf of Guinea, on the African coast, runs westerly across the Atlantic, and through the Carribean Sea, enters the Gulf of Mexico. The circuit is complete, you see. And the waters, constantly rounding this vast circuit, as constantly throw off into the still water of the centre, all the floating material that they accumulate—just as in the pail, the *moving* waters reject the bits of wood, and they go inevitably into the quiet place in the centre.

Now place the point of your pencil on the Bermuda Islands, then move it east across the ocean to the Azores, then south to the Cape de Verde Islands, then back across the ocean to the Bermudas again. Nearly within the triangular limits you have described the Sargasso Sea lies. It is about 260,000 square miles in extent.

The greatest masses of weed are found at the north-west and south-east extremities, one near the Bermudas, the other just west of the Canaries. It was in the neighborhood of this latter place that we now were.

Humboldt has named this floating weed the "Tropic Grape"—botanists term it *fucus natans*. It grows upon submarine rocks, from the Equator to the fortieth parallel of latitude.

In contemplating one of these great masses, a variety almost infinite in form and extent is presented to the eye. I do not mean variety in the masses, but in the weeds that compose them. The most frequent is the short, branchy cluster, so common in the Gulf Stream. There is one kind, however, described as having a stem from 1,000 to 1,500 feet in length, of the size of one's finger, and with "filaments branching upwards like packthread."

This sea is also very prolific of animal life. Indeed, naturalists describe it as consisting in part of minute organisms. These afford food to larger creatures, that are in their own turn devoured.

The Medusæ journey thither from the Gulf of Mexico and fatten on the spoil they take—and the whale also journeys thither; and as he is very fond of the Medusæ (they are his principal food), and finds them here fat and tender, we can imagine what their fate is.

The Medusæ, commonly called *sea nettles*, are a jelly-like substance, having the head, or what answers to the head, in the centre, and the other members radiating from this head.

The mass of weed I have described was the largest that we saw, and with the leading breeze that we then had, it soon disappeared on the quarter.

This Sargasso Sea is not only an interesting locality to naturalists, but also to the classical student, and the student of mediæval literature.

Here the Atlantis of Plato was located, that land of grain and wine, and olives, of mighty forests, green pastures, and splendid cities. Here, too, were the Fortunate Islands, with their salubrious climate, and profusion of perennial flowers. Here rose the Isles of the Blessed, where the righteous, without tasting death, realized heaven and immortal bliss.

Here, at a later day, men looked for the Isle of St. Borondon, whose mountains loomed so enchantingly to the eye, and yet so constantly eluded all near approach.

Here, too, was the Island of the Seven Cities, with its population of true believers, and its cross-crowned churches, inviting worship.

How the human soul, longing with inexpressible

desire for the lost Eden of the race, luxuriates in these descriptions of imaginary abodes of rest and peace!

In the appendix to his Life of Columbus, Washington Irving gives very interesting accounts of the Islands of St. Borondon and the Seven Cities.

I said these accounts were interesting,—so is the whole work. For every one who has not read it, there is a great treat in reserve, and I recommend partaking of it as soon as convenient.

My habit of deserting my work to see what was going on, of course called forth remonstrances from the steward. I heard them unmoved, never promising to do better, and never making any offensive reply—I may as well say never making *any* reply, for I never did—but I continued steadfastly to do as before.

At length the case was laid before the captain. The result was that I was ignominiously dismissed, and a Bath boy, a year or two older, appointed in my place.

I now became, in some respects, a vagabond—*i. e.*, I experienced all the joys of vagabond life, without any of its hardships and discomforts. I slept very cosily at night, and feasted, physically and mentally, by day. My physical food was pea soup, beef, and duff—my mental food such books as "Ten Thousand Topsail-Sheet Blocks," "Fanny Campbell,

The Female Pirate Captain," and "The Blood-Red Revenger of the Spanish Main." This kind of literature the passengers possessed by the bushel.

These books were enclosed in fair "yellow covers," and on their pages, inside, were described adventures so wonderful that sometimes doubts of their truth rose, even in my confiding mind. It was all *in print*, however, and my doubts could not scale such a wall as that. Many men disbelieve that "Whatever is, is right," but no natural child disbelieves that *whatever is in print, is true.*

As my supplies of time and books were unlimited, I read on, and on, and on, until, at length, I got an overdose, and became violently sick of "yellow covered literature." Even now, when I see such books, the sight produces nausea.

Many men are miserable because their children seem to have acquired an insatiable taste for reading "dime novels." The taste is *not* insatiable, thou unhappy parent, but can be corrected. How are children cured of stealing sugar? Not by any Homeopathic doses, but by being compelled to eat sugar in great quantities, until the stomach rebels, and sends the saccharine matter back by the way it came. Really, though if not Homeopathic practice, this is Homeopathic principle—*similia similibus curantur.*

Proceed in the same way to correct this taste

for reading these books that are morally and mentally injurious. Buy dime novels by the wholesale, set the children to reading, keep them reading; when they tire give them no rest, and, my word for it, in the end, you may cow them by the name of these books, as "on the sands of Yemen the Arab mother hushed her child by the name of Richard."

CHAPTER VII.

THE TRADE WINDS.—"MAN OVERBOARD."—EL GOLFO DE LAS DAMAS.

READER, I must ask you to resort to your Atlas again. Open to the map of the world. I propose to state the general rule in regard to winds. The Equator is the centre of a calm space, called the Equatorial Belt of calm. This belt is six degrees in width, and, the Equator, being the centre, of course three degrees are of north latitude, and three of south.

This is not exactly true all the year round, for the belt is influenced by the sun as it declines to the north and south. But my design is to present the *general* rule only.

Between the northern degree of this belt, and the thirtieth parallel of north latitude, the trade winds blow continually.

Between the thirtieth and thirty-fifth parallels of north latitude, is the calm belt of Cancer, called by the sailors "the horse latitudes." Here the calms are varied by light, shifting winds.

From this calm belt of Cancer to the northern limit of navigation, south-west and west winds prevail.

Going south from the calm belt of the Equator, we have first the region of the south-east trade winds. This region extends to the thirtieth parallel of south latitude, and then comes the calm belt of Capricorn. From this calm belt to the south pole westerly winds prevail.

A knowledge of these facts just stated was obtained by years of observation.

Now for the theory. In presenting it I will make my explanations as brief as possible.

The atmosphere of the torrid zone, rarified by the greater amount of heat, rises.

The air from both poles rushes in to fill the vacuum. The result of that would be north and south winds, blowing from the respective poles to the Equator.

But this result is modified—

1. By the rotary motion of the earth about its axis. It is easy to see that this easterly progress of the earth would give a westerly direction to the north and south currents. It produces that change in them which gives us the north-east and south-east trade winds.

2. A return current from the Equator towards

the poles, interferes with a regular and uninterrupted flow of the air from the poles to the Equator.

While the polar atmosphere rushes to the Equator, the equatorial atmosphere rushes to the poles to fill the vaccuum there. It is but an exchange of places.

The rarified air of the equatorial region moves north and south *above* the currents moving in the opposite directions. Gradually increasing in density as it recedes from the torrid zone, it descends, and meets the polar currents between the thirtieth and thirty-fifth parallels of latitude, and this meeting produces the calm belts of Cancer and Capricorn.

In the struggle here the relative positions of the opposing currents are changed. That which moves to the north becomes the lower current, and that which moves toward the south the upper.

This wonderful circulation is incessant; this going forth, and returning, admits no pause in the start, or on the home-stretch. This circulation preserves for the atmosphere its tonic, exhilarating, life-giving power.

It is not a bad theory, is it? Certain it is that we cannot adopt it, without an increase of our love and reverence for the Great Creator.

It was the design of my father at the outset of the voyage, to touch at the Cape Verde Islands for water and fresh provisions. But, when within three hundred miles of them, to the north-west, we struck the fresh trade winds from the east-north-east.

Braced sharp up we could just look up for the Islands. The ship was crank, the sea heavy, and the current adverse. Under these circumstances to fetch these Islands was impossible, and, as there was sufficient water on board, it was resolved to keep the ship off for Rio Janeiro, in Brazil.

This was October fifth.

The first part of the evening I was upon deck. Everybody was in high spirits. There was reason for it. We were making wonderful progress. The wind was aft the beam, so that the great crowd of sail that was carried on the ship drew fairly. The foretopmast studding-sail was set with a brace upon the boom. The sea was long and high. Now and then a wave would rear its crest far up and break. I could see it for a moment, gleaming with ghostly whiteness out in the night, then it would go down with a sudden plunge, scattering the white foam far ahead. Overhead the stars were gleaming through a hazy atmosphere. Far astern the path of the ship was marked with phosphorescent light. The scene was exhilarating, and I enjoyed it long.

At length I descended to the cabin and stretched myself on the transom locker that I have described. My father and several of the after-cabin passengers were about the table, playing whist. It might have been half an hour from the time when I came into the cabin, that I heard a loud, but not intelligible shout from the forward part of the ship. The whist players paused in all the attitudes of the game, and, with their heads inclined, seemed to listen painfully for a repetition of the cry. It came, almost immediately, and this time from the poop deck above our heads. I did not even then understand the words, but I saw the group at the table drop their cards, with one motion, and leaping up, rush upon deck.

Filled with astonishment, I also hastened to the companion way and ascended. At first I beheld only a dim mass of human forms, tossing in the wildest confusion; then I saw forward through the dusky air the foretopmast studding sail, with tack gone, flaunting like a great battle banner from the yard. The weather leeches of the topsails were lifting, and away up, almost out of sight in the gloom, I could hear the flutter of the lighter canvass.

I walked aft. The man at the wheel was turning it to port, tugging at the spokes with might and main. The ship was flying away obliquely across the sea several points from her course.

"Who is overboard?" roared my father from the neighborhood of the mizzen-mast.

Then it was out. Then first I knew why all these things were done.

"Who is overboard?" my father had demanded.

The hubbub of human voices, which had hitherto been deafening, died away, and one or two tongues replied promptly:

"The steward—the steward!"

"How came he there?"

"He jumped over."

"Was the alarm given immediately?"

"No, not for five or ten minutes. We didn't believe he was gone at first."

There was a pause, then my father spoke again.

"We are at least two miles from the man. The sea runs high, and to send out the boat to look for him would be to endanger the lives of all in her without a chance of saving his. Besides, he jumped overboard. Neither reason nor humanity requires a boat's crew to be risked in search of him. Haul out that tack again."

It was all over. It only remained to discuss the event. Gradually, as the discussion went on, the facts were brought out.

The steward had been accused of taking liquor from the state rooms of the passengers, and drinking it. This he strenuously denied, and also made the gratuitous assertion that he never used intoxicating drinks. But the liquor still continued to disappear, and the steward was often observed to be in a very excited state, raving almost, and then to become ill. Just previous to his jumping overboard he was thus excited, and at night grew sick. Dr. Burleigh, who still suspected him of theft and drunkenness, determined upon a plan to satisfy himself in regard to it. Therefore, when the man was much distressed, he gave him a powerful emetic, and desired him to deposit whatever he raised in a bucket which he brought to him. A man was placed to watch him, and see that he did not cast the contents of the bucket overboard.

He soon vomited, and then he rose and walked out of the cabin. Seeing that he left the bucket behind, the man who was on the watch did not interfere with his motions.

Having reached the deck, the steward walked past a number of passengers, who were sitting on the main hatch, chatting, and going to the starboard side of the deck, climbed up over the rail. Hanging by his hands, and one foot over the water, he turned his face towards those on the hatch, said deliberately — "Good night, gentlemen," and disappeared.

Those to whom he spoke, supposing him to be in sport, and still hanging on outside of the rail, did not trouble themselves about him at first. But when five minutes, or more, had gone by, and he did not reappear, they began to feel uneasy.

And when, on looking, they could not discover him, they gave the alarm, and pitched overboard the carpenter's work-bench and a hen-coop.

The mate, when he heard the cry, without a moment's thought, ordered the helm to be put hard-a-starboard, and sprang to the boat to cast off her lashings.

At this moment my father reached the deck. Seeing in what jeopardy the spars stood, he ordered the helm to be changed at once, and the studding-sail tack let go. These orders were promptly obeyed, and the ship saved from catching aback.

What followed has already been told.

With regard to the contents of the bucket, my memory has failed me. I have a dim impression that brandy was there, but I will not say that it was so.

The man was a strange one. The name he went by was evidently not his own.

There were various reasons assigned for his rash act. Some thought he did not intend to get clear overboard, and that his climbing over the side was a sort of crazy joke.

But the greater number were more uncharitable, and hinted about delirium tremens.

On former occasions he had threatened to jump overboard.

The old Spanish navigators, in crossing from the old world to the new, did not steer directly across the ocean, but ran south, down the African coast (cutting the Tropic of Cancer just to the westward of the Cape Verde Islands), until they reached about the fifteenth parallel of latitude, and then, turning to the west, made a straight course across.

In this latitude the trade winds blow more directly from the east, and the water is stiller, and the skies brighter. The ship runs day after day without a change in the sails.

Humboldt compares crossing the ocean here, to descending a smoothly flowing river, and considers there is less danger than in crossing one of the lakes of Switzerland.

The Spaniards called it *El Golfo de las Damas*, the Ladies' Gulf, as much as to say that delicate and sensitive women might navigate it with perfect freedom from sea-sickness.

As we ran on to the south, the strength of the wind gradually lessened. The sea fell, till the motion of the ship was hardly perceptible.

Universal nature has been termed a vast book, from which all in sympathy with nature can read.

The page open to us then, was inscribed with poetry—the poetry of the sea. Whoso loved poesy and read:

> * * "To him the gushing of the wave,
> Far, far away did seem to mourn and rave
> On alien shores; * * * *
> And deep asleep he seemed, yet all awake,
> And music in his ears his beating heart did make."

Great whales swam leisurely by, projecting their spiral columns of water into the air, and occasionally displaying their vast black bulk to view. The swift dolphins glided in our wake. We caught them, and gazed with wonder on the rainbow colors which they assumed in the agonies of death. The petrel twittered about the stern. Shoals of porpoises frisked about the bow, mocking our best speed. At times, the man-eating shark ominously broke water on the quarters. We caught the Portugese man-of-war, and burned our fingers in our eager curiosity. Clouds of flying fish rose before our advancing ship, like grasshoppers, in autumn, before the pedestrian. Far up, the tropic bird floated in the blue ether. Day succeeded night, and night the day, and always—

> "The sun came up upon the left,
> Out of the sea came he,
> And he shone bright, and on the right
> Went down into the sea."

CHAPTER VIII.

IN THE DOLDRUMS.—CAPTURE OF A SHARK.—SHARKS.
—THE SOUTHERN HEMISPHERE.

WE exchanged the delightful navigation of the trade wind region, for the vexatious navigation of the calm belt of the Equator, the *doldrums* of the sailor. It was a poor exchange, but necessary.

> "Day after day, day after day,
> We stuck, nor breath nor motion,
> As idle as a painted ship
> Upon a painted ocean."

That was the Ancient Mariner's ship, mind you, that *stuck* in such a melancholy manner. We stuck often enough, and long enough at a time, but there was some life and motion—some of that variety which is "the spice of life." There were more or less squalls. A black cloud would rise in some part of the great blue dome that enclosed us, and precipitated itself upon the ship in wind and rain.

Generally, though, there were "several rains to one wind," as the boys say. However, there was always enough of the latter to make it necessary to trim sails, a task that could hardly be executed before both rain and wind were passed. Out would blaze again the fierce sun. Wet shirts dried speedily on the backs of the wearers. The wet on the decks rose in exhalations, and soon the pitch in the seams, which had been boiling and bubbling before, would boil and bubble again.

This state of things continued several days, and a history of one day is a history of all.

To the discomfort of intense heat, was added the hardship of very poor water. It had been filled from the Kennebec, and was none too good at the time of filling. That was bad. It was put into casks that had never held water before. That was bad, too. Down there on the line it had become ropy. It would string up on a stick like molasses. When one took it *raw*, it was necessary to hold the nose tightly with one hand, and shut the eyes. The sense of taste was still left to come in contact with it, it is true, but thirst would overcome the disgust of that.

There is an idea prevalent among sea-faring people, that whistling in a calm will bring wind. Absurd as this may seem, it is true. If the whistling is continued *long enough*, the wind will surely come. We whistled zealously, but after two or three days it got to be rather tiresome, and we hailed with joy the advent of a shark that swam leisurely and inquiringly up to the ship, probably with the mistaken notion that we were an African slaver, and could supply—would be happy to do so—a dinner of smothered negroes to an itinerant shark. Besides the usual obsequious pilot fish, there was a train of young sharks in attendance.

Something was soon prepared for the visitor, but it was not food. The third mate got into the mizzen channels, under which the shark was lying, and presented his compliments in the shape of a harpoon, which he drove half way through the unsuspicious fish. And then there occurred before the eyes of many witnesses, something which, I see, is not credited in learned descriptions of the shark. This was a female, and no sooner was the iron fixed in her than, as if apprehensive of harm to them, she received the young sharks into her stomach.

Nothing gives a sailor more pleasure than to destroy a shark; therefore but little time elapsed after the monster had been struck, before a bowline was over the tail, and madame shark was escorted to the port gangway. Here all hands were drawn up to do her honor (or spite), and her passage from the water to the deck, was attended by all the tumult that three score tongues could make.

Once upon the deck, madame began to apply her tail to it in a way that shook the ship. A man thereupon seized an axe, and sprang forward to sever the unruly member—the tail—from the body; but Dr. Burleigh, who was very much excited, withheld him.

"On the head," said he. "Hit her on the head. I want to examine this tail, and see how so much power is developed."

So the head received what was designed for the tail, and under a torrent of blows (each one accompanied by an anathema), the shark seemed to succumb. The Doctor then approached, and began an examination of the caudal appendage, remarking excitedly and learnedly to those around him as he proceeded:

"Notice how this tail is bent up here at an obtuse angle with the body. And see this tail fin. How distinct its divisions into three parts! Naturalists call them, I think, the superior, apical, and inferior lobes. But look at this part of the tail again. Feel of it. Talk of human brawn and sinew. Why, in the cartilaginous bone and solid flesh of this shark, there's more power and endurance than—"

Here the defunct (supposed to be) shark, as if to give an illustration of the truth of the Doctor's remarks, suddenly struck that individual a blow with her tail, as he leaned over, heaving him backwards into the arms of his hearers, with his stomach collapsed, and his head in close contact with his knees.

And then, while the naturalist had no breath left with which to offer an objection, (if he still had the disposition, which may be doubted,) the assault with the axe was renewed, and the tail nearly severed from the body in several places.

The throat was then cut, and the stomach opened. Out of this, seven young sharks were taken, "alive and well." They were about twenty inches in length, and, on a small scale, fine models of their mother.

The axe was immediately applied to them, and they were each thrown overboard in two pieces. And then the old shark, beaten on the head, disembowelled, with throat cut, and tail chopped off, was cast, with scoffs and revilings, after her young. Life *ought* to have been extinct under these circumstances, but it was not. No sooner had the water closed over her, than she assumed a life-like position—the pectoral fins beat the water feebly, and the body moved languidly away.

I think, however, despite the tenacity of life, that there was, at no remote time, the corpse of a shark in those waters.

I have some hesitation about assigning our prize to any particular branch of the shark family. It resembled in color the blue shark, but it exceeded the individuals of that species in size, and the tropics are not a favorite locality of the blue shark.

The animal we had killed was upwards of twelve feet in length. Its snout projected beyond its mouth, which was capacious, and displayed the liberal allowance of triangular, serrated teeth, which has fallen to the lot of sharks. And "its eyes had all the seeming of a demon's that is dr—" no, *not* dreaming, but wide awake, and engaged in a most fiendish piece of cruelty. There is something absolutely diabolical in the gaze of a shark. The skin was rough as a grater, and hard. Sharks have no scales.

The white shark is the most formidable of the species, though it is often surpassed in size by the basking shark, a specimen of which kind, it will be remembered, was captured recently near Eastport, in Maine.

The white shark attains a length of thirty or thirty-five feet. Its belly and sides are whitish, and its back brown. Its head is large, and its mouth enormous. It frequents the tropics, swimming near the surface.

The story goes that this kind of shark used to attend the slave ships on their return from Africa with cargoes of slaves. Old sailors credit it with great intelligence in the matter, and say it fully comprehends the state of affairs on board.

The sperm whale is the only inhabitant of the ocean that can destroy the white shark in a fair combat. The whale, not being properly a fish, the title of "King of the Fishes," may be said to belong rightfully to the white shark.

The swingle-tail, or fox shark, the hammer-headed shark, and the saw-fish, represent the uncouth and remarkable of the shark family.

I would like to tell a shark story here, but I realize that I am progressing slowly on the long road I propose to travel, and I refrain.

October 5th we fanned across the equinoxial line, and entered the Southern Hemisphere. Here, midway across the torrid zone, I would pause a moment to remark upon its characteristics. It is here that a wanderer from the far North is most sensible of a new order of things. Perpetual summer reigns. To distant lands, grim winter with his frost and snow, is exiled evermore. The North wind is shorn of its sting. The Sun is King supreme.

But more strange to him than constant summer, is the aspect of the sky; for in his own land there is summer once a year, and balmy air, and glorious sunshine; but his eyes raised to the starry vault behold no Southern Cross, no Constellation of the Ship, no Magellanic Clouds.

Just think of it—before us was an unknown firmament, set with new and splendid Constellations and stars, and behind us, what? A lonesome spectacle, a northern firmament without a polar star.

Another peculiarity, to us, of this region, was

the sudden transition from light to darkness, and from darkness to light, at the setting, and the rising of the sun. Here, in the north, the sun, as it were, comes slowly up. We see first a faint glow of light low down along the east. Slowly it widens and brightens, flushing up the sky. Dark objects change to gray, and gray to white. One by one the stars go out; and at length, the sun, too bright for human eyes to gaze upon, appears, throwing a flood of light on the hill tops and into the valleys.

In the intertropical region it is not so. There the sun *leaps* above the horizon, and the change from darkness to light is instantaneous and complete. No crepuscular light intervenes, as here, to introduce the divisions of time to each other. The change from light to darkness is equally swift.

> "The sun's rim dips; the stars rush out;
> At one stride comes the dark—"

Particularly was this the case when we reached the fourteenth parallel of south latitude, which represented the sun's southern declination at that time.

At noon the great orb was exactly overhead and we cast no shadows. And thereafter, until we had doubled on our course, and reached the torrid zone again in the Pacific, the sun's path lay to the north of us.

There is a rare beauty about a "sunset at sea" in the tropics. The clouds, absent all day, then gather in the West, sometimes in fleecy fragments. They catch the bright rays, flung broadcast from the sinking luminary, and present them again to the eye in gorgeous colors, or in those soft tints and hues, that the highest human genius must always fail to represent on canvass.

Sunsets, at sea, in every clime, have a wide reputation for beauty. Early on the passage my attention was drawn to this fact by hearing the passengers comment upon it.

And I soon learned how to behold three sunsets at the close of one day. I would stand on deck until the sun went down and out of sight, and I had beheld the spectacle once, then I would spring into the rigging and go rapidly aloft. Before reaching the topsail yard, my elevation would be sufficient to make the sun again visible above the horizon. As soon as it had set a second time, I would rapidly ascend again with the same result as before. This was a favorite amusement with me until I tired of it.

CHAPTER IX.

FERNANDO NORONHA.—A SUSPICIOUS SAIL.—RIO JANEIRO.

October 27th, two days after crossing the line, we made the Island of Fernando Noronha. We saw it first in the morning, bearing west-south-west, distant twenty-five miles. I sat upon the mizzen topgallant yard, and gazed at it for hours. Since the shores of Maine disappeared, we had seen no other land. This was in another hemisphere, and in the torrid zone. Of course I was very happy, sitting aloft and beholding Fernando Noronha, as we glided slowly by it. A wall of white foam girdled the dark, high shore. It seemed noiseless and motionless, but I knew it was rolling and dashing with a noise like thunder; so far off were we that neither motion was distinguishable, nor noise audible. Though the wall of foam appeared a straight unbroken line against the land, not so the land against the sky. The tall pyramid, which renders the appearance of the Island remarkable, shot up like the spire of a church.

Fernando Noronha lies about 200 miles from the coast of Brazil, in 3° 55′ south latitude. It is seven miles long, and three broad.

The pyramid is about 1000 feet in height, and composed of phonolitic rocks, severed, in many places, into irregular columns.

Another freak of nature, also, is seen on this Island. Its south-west point is pierced through, and the aperture has received the name of the "Hole-in-the-Wall." Through it the sea tumbles magnificently.

Fernando Noronha is well wooded. The soil is generally fertile; but, on two accounts, not much is produced from it. Frequent and long droughts is one reason, and the other is a lack of energy and enterprise in the inhabitants.

The Brazilian government has made the Island a place of exile for the vilest criminals. It is garrisoned by a small force, and has been fortified to some extent.

In most accounts of this Island it is stated that no woman is allowed to set her foot upon it.

If this were true we might fancy that old bachelors would commit crimes in order to be banished thither. But, fortunately for all its people, convicts and keepers, this is not true. Capt. Lee, of the U. S. brig Dolphin, gives the following list of population in 1852, viz., 103 officers and soldiers, 310 prisoners, 289 other persons, men, *women*, and children.

I remember that I had resolved to sketch all the wonderful lands we should see. It was a most presumptious resolution, for I could not then, cannot now, and never can sketch any more than a horse. But I began, and sketched Fernando Noronha. My sketch might be called a kind of a fresco, for I lay in my berth and used the pencil on the wall.

The *black place* that I made still remained when, at the end of the voyage, I left the ship, and as its value would hardly justify any one in carrying off the board it was on, it probably there remained until, together with hull and cargo, spars, sails and rigging, it was buried beneath the ocean in the grave where so many ships lie.

We passed Fernando Noronha with a light wind from the south-east. This continued two or three days, during which we ran close hauled by the wind on a south-south-west course.

One night during that time, I was aroused by hearing hoarse voices, shouting, and unintelligible words. I got out of my berth very expeditiously, and a few steps placed me in position to make observations. It was a fine starlight night, and I saw, as soon as I had rubbed my eyes open, just under our lee, two towering pyramids of canvass rising in the air. The hull from which they rose was hardly distinguishable, but their rake, and a long succession of jibs, in one direction, indicated that the stranger was sailing in the same direction as ourselves. The hailing that had aroused me was still going on, though the usual questions had been asked and answered.

"How many passengers did you say you had?" asked the voice from the brig.

The number was given a second time, and then followed statements of longitude, and histories of wind and weather.

Notwithstanding that she was directly under our lee, and her sails somewhat becalmed by ours, the brig drew rapidly ahead, and was soon hidden from view aft, by our head sails.

"What brig is it?" I asked of one of the watch.

"Blamed if I could understand what he called her. What was it, Tom?" he asked of another sailor.

"Don't know." And the question passed around, eliciting from all the men the same reply, accompanied in some cases by the information that the stranger was "from St. Johns, loaded with codfish, and bound to Pernambuco, and could everlastingly sail."

So I ascended to the poop deck, and insinuated my questions there. But no more knowledge was to be gained there than on the main deck. I then looked into the binnacle, and seeing that it was only half-past three, A. M., turned in again, and was soon dreaming of a nameless brig "from St. Johns, loaded with codfish, and bound to Pernambuco, and that could everlastingly sail."

The sun was shining brightly over the vast expanse of ocean, when, at seven bells, I stepped on deck again. The brig was a mile or two ahead and behaved oddly, everybody said.

It *was* odd behavior. She would sweep up to the wind, and lie with sails shaking a while, and then, having gathered way again, she would yaw broad off, and run before the wind a few minutes. Her aim in this was, evidently, not to increase her distance from us.

At ten she wore short round on her heel, and stood back, heading just to leeward of us.

Then I began to hear the word *pirate* used pretty freely. The popular description of a piratical craft applied to her exactly. She was long, low in the water, and her black paint was relieved only by a narrow yellow stripe. Her masts were long and raked a great deal, and her sails were large and many.

I soon found out, (for my own fears were excited, and I put a great many questions), there were two classes that said *pirate*. One class really thought the stranger to be a freebooter; the other class did not think so, but pretended to, and said and did all they could to create a panic. The mate was one of the latter class. His state room was at the side of one of the entrances to the cabin from the main deck. Pretty soon those passing in and out, saw through the door of the room, purposely left open, his sword and pistols lying on the table. This fact was soon noised abroad, and was considered terribly ominous.

Another of this class, an old sailor, who was a kind of oracle to many of the passengers, borrowed a spyglass of the officers, and ascended with it to the foretopsail yard. From thence he made a long and close scrutiny of the brig, now under our lee again, about a quarter of a mile off.

When he came down he was immediately surrounded by anxious passengers. His countenance was portentous.

"Load your rifles and pistols," he said, nodding his head significantly, "and get ready to die like men. It'll come to that, or walking a plank."

"What did you see?" gasped several.

"Codfish be blowed—" he said, looking absently into the air, and then turning to the questioners, he answered:

"Why, the hatches are all open, and I saw them, and the gangways, full of heads with red caps on. And," pointing his finger toward the brig, "do you see that whitish bunch just aft the foremast?"

I could see nothing, but others seemed to have better eyes, for there was a chorus of "Yes, yes!"

"Well, I saw the top of that bunch lifted, and if there ain't a long brass thirty-two pounder under there, call me a swab, that's all."

Saying this, he turned away, leaving his hearers in rather an uncomfortable frame of mind.

When the brig was off our lee quarter, our colors were hoisted. None were shown in return. I looked at her frequently with the glass. Her decks were flush, but I saw nothing unusual on them. Besides the man at the wheel, there were a few others sauntering about the deck. That was all.

As the brig increased her distance from us, the terrified ones began to breathe more freely. One even said, in a joking way, to the oracular sailor:

"Well, your pirate seems to be taking himself off, after all."

The man answered with terrible positiveness, and deliberation:

"Mark my words. In ten minutes that fellow will be round in our wake, and then if he don't open with *long Tom*, and make toothpicks of us, just get ready to repel boarders, that's all."

In two minutes from that time the brig tacked, and came on with her head straight for us.

A great many loaded their firearms. On one poor fellow, insane with fear, the sailors tied, with a rope yarn, an old rusty cutlass, and put on his head a canvass draw-bucket, adorned with a rooster's tail feathers. Thus accoutred he ran about the deck in a perfect frenzy.

But the terrible brig, as she neared us, hugged the wind closer and closer, and passed a mile, or more, to windward. When the sun went down she was hull down on our weather bow.

The forecastle oracle, however, insisted that she would be down upon us again in the night, and, through his representations, many were robbed of their sleep. But when morning came the suspicious craft was nowhere to be seen.

It must be conceded that the manœuvres of this vessel were mysterious, if not suspicious. During the day it was the opinion of our officers that Capt. John Bull (the brig had claimed to be English) had uncorked some very strong ale that morning, and was giving "the blasted Yankee a specimen of British sailing, you know." But her final disappearance, on a wind, when her port lay to leeward, combined with all the rest, inclined them to think her an outward bound slaver, in want of provisions. Probably our large number of passengers prevented our being boarded and plundered.

Nov. 6, at noon, we made the lofty promontory of Cape Frio, bearing west, distant forty-five miles During the afternoon, the wind was light, and we made but little headway. Towards night, however, it freshened, and the ship, bending gracefully to it, dashed along with great swiftness.

Just before sunset an object was discovered shoreward of us, rising and falling on the waves. It seemed to be a small sail, but what it was spread upon we could not imagine. As the course of the ship was almost directly towards it, and the wind fresh, we soon had it close aboard.

It was a queer craft. The hull consisted of logs fastened together. The single mast raised near what was then the bow, and crossed at the top by a yard from which the dingy sail hung like a ship's foresail. There appeared to be a raised seat at the other end that accommodated the crew of two men. The swiftly coming darkness did not permit us to note many particulars, but we saw enough to know that this was a jangada, or catamaran, a kind of craft used by the Brazilians in fishing and coasting.

These catamarans are generally composed of from eight to twelve trunks of the buoyant, jangada tree, rudely secured by wooden cross-fastenings. The more common sail is a triangular, fore and aft one. We should not wish to navigate our coasts with such contrivances, but it is a different thing along the Brazilian shore.

There the winds are as constant as the sun, at night, and in the morning, blowing off shore, and during the day blowing on shore. These are called land and sea breezes. They are caused by the sun's heat by day, and the absence of that heat at night. The earth is sooner heated by the sun's rays than the water, and the rarified air ascends. The cooler air from the ocean, rushing shoreward to fill the vacuum, makes the *sea breeze*.

The earth cools more rapidly than the water, in the absence of the sun's rays, and consequently at night and in the morning there is a passage of air from the land to the water. This makes the *land breeze*.

When the sun rose the following morning, we were becalmed off the entrance to the Bay of Rio Janeiro. The ship was all alive. Expectation stood upon tiptoe. Here, a group of passengers stood gazing upon the lofty brown summits of the mountains, and discussing their appearance in cheerful and animated tones—there, others were blacking their boots and brushing their coats preparatory to examining more closely this novel and majestic land.

Forward the crew were hooking up the chain cables from their lockers, overhauling ranges, and casting loose the anchors. Aft the boys were scouring up the brass ornaments, and rubbing the tarnish from the white paint.

Vessels were all around, inside and outside, wherever the land breeze had failed them.

Ever and anon, over the sparkling expanse of water, that stretched away inland, came the hoarse boom of cannon. It was a time of joyous excitement until the wind came; a time of eager anticipation, yet of high enjoyment.

About noon a movement in the air was perceptible. The light sails began to flutter; the smooth surface of the water stirred, and the sea breeze was setting in.

Hardly fifteen minutes had elapsed, after the first faint breath, before we were gliding quickly along with every sail fairly filled and distended by the breeze.

I gazed in admiration and awe. On the left was the Pao d'Ossucar, the Sugar Loaf, which forms the west side of the entrance to the bay, and is a certain and unmistakable landmark.

My eyes took in, at once, its perfectly conical sides, so steep and smooth, and beyond it a range of fantastic hills, receding one behind another until lost in the distance. On the right hand were less lofty hills, clad with tropical vegetation. We could distinguish the broad leaf of the banana and the feathery foliage of the palm.

The first fortification we passed was the Castle of Santa Cruz, situated at the eastern extremity of the entrance. Between this and Ilha da Lage opposite, the passage is only about 5,000 feet in width.

The castle was a vast and massive structure. Great cannons stared at us over the front wall, and from a tall staff above them streamed the Brazilian flag.

A sentinel paced the battlements, wheeling in his rounds right above the seething foam, that frothed and frittered on the rocks below, for the castle wall rose, as it were, sharply up from the edge of the sea. We passed within a stone's throw of it. The sentinel hailed in bad English:

"What sheep is dat?"

"The Hampton."

"Vare well. Where you come from?"

"Bath, U. S. A."

"Vare well. Where you go?"

"San Francisco."

"Vare well. I tank you, sare."

This last was said with a wave of the hand, as if to say—"Pass, ship Hampton."

And now the whole magnificent Bay of Rio Janeiro opened before us. With many a gradual curve, and many a sharp angle, the right hand shore swept away to the north. On the left, battery after battery watched defiantly the incoming and outgoing ships.

Beyond lay the city, at the feet of the mountains, its streets wandering in the valleys, and its churches and convents crowning the summits of the hills. The sharp, high peaks of the Organ Mountains, a fitting background to so fine a picture, closed the view in that direction. Off from the city was the anchorage crowded with ships, the men-of-war by themselves in one place, the merchantmen by themselves in another. At 4 P. M. we anchored.

CHAPTER X.

AT RIO JANEIRO.

NO sooner had the ship swung to her anchor, than a number of boats approached within speaking distance, and their occupants, lying on their oars, entered into conversation with us. They were ship-chandlers, and offered to furnish for the ship whatever was required.

The truth of the old saying, "Two of a trade can never agree," was here exemplified, as strongly as ever it was in the northern hemisphere. The rival merchants designated each other by the most opprobrious epithets, and bandied words in a manner not surpassed by the ancient dames of any fish-market in the world. They were generally Englishmen.

In the midst of the parley a man-of-war's boat, rowed by eight men, steered by a coxswain, commanded by a midshipman, and flying the stars and stripes, pulled up, and lay on our starboard quarter. The midshipman hailed in very polite tones, beginning with the question, "What ship is that?" and ending with, "Have you seen any ships of the squadron."

We had not seen any.

To a question from us, he replied that he belonged to the frigate "Brandywine," flag-ship of the United States squadron on the Brazilian station. This fine frigate was easily distinguished, lying among the armed ships of many nations, in the direction of the Island of Cobras.

As the boat sped away, the eight oars dipping with the exactness of machinery, it was followed by very envious looks from me, directed chiefly at the youthful officer, whose gold lace and dignified occupation fascinated me.

In due time the port formalities were over, and boats were permitted to come alongside, and we were at liberty to go on shore. Then a ship-chandler was engaged to supply the ship.

I believe the applicant who received the most abuse from his fellows was the one favored with our custom. This was done, I suppose, on the principle that "the devil is never so black as he is painted."

This man entered upon his duties by immediately bringing off to the ship, as a present (he said), several bushels of oranges and bananas.

That night it fell to my lot to stand anchor

watch from eight to ten. I passed the two hours in a very agreeable manner, eating oranges, and listening to the music of the bands on board the men-of-war.

It seems to me that the most unappreciative nature would have enjoyed that evening, even without the oranges.

The air was delicious. The starry host were making their finest display. The surface of the water was like a mirror—like it, in that it was smooth as glass, and in that it reflected all the overhanging stars.

The lights of the city, beginning high up among the dark hills, swept down to the water's edge, and seemed to be continued on in the lights of the shipping

Beyond, the dark outlines of the mountains were dimly visible, in seeming, a mighty rampart, bristling with towers, and guarding the city to the west.

In the opposite directions, across the bay, fewer and less distinct, the lights of Praia Grande and San Domingo were visible.

While the sense of sight was thus addressed, the hearing was ravished by the strains of music that came, purified by their passage, over the intervening water.

I landed two or three times each day, but was generally left in charge of the boat, and my chances for observation were very limited. But one day I was relieved from this duty, and it was with great joy that I turned my back upon the landing, and set forward to "see what I should see."

A little way from the shore I lingered at the threshold of a large building, inside of which, in full view, scores of naval officers, English, American, French, Spanish, and Brazilian, all gorgeous in bullion, lace, and glittering trappings, were smoking, chatting, and playing billiards.

At every onward step some novelty greeted my senses.

Troops of stalwart negroes, with sacks of coffee on their heads, trotted in Indian file along the streets, shouting, singing, and shaking rattles as they went.

I heard no intelligible sound from any source.

My eyes rested wonderingly on the white stone walls, and red tiled roofs of the buildings. And the style of architecture was new and strange. But what drew admiration as well as wonder from me was beholding the marvelous fountains. They abound in the city. Many that I saw were designed mainly as monuments are with us; a square base supporting a shaft. From the four sides of this base poured streams of sparkling water, that fell into reservoirs, from which it was dipped and drank, or conveyed away, as required. The faces of the base were tastefully sculptured, and there was a style about the shafts that seemed Arabesque, and there are reasons why it might have been so.

At these reservoirs multitudes of blacks of both sexes were filling, amid shouts of laughter and the shrillest ejaculations, vessels with water, and conveying them away upon their heads.

At length I reached the market, and not Aladin when he surveyed the treasures of that subterranean treasure house, was more amazed than I, on this occasion.

Parrots displayed their gay plumage and uttered their harsh screams. Hosts of diminutive monkeys gyrated and chattered. Over a vast space boquets of fresh and beautiful flowers filled the air with fragrance. Green vegetables and bright yellow fruits were mingled in a pleasing contrast. Portly negresses, turbaned and dignified, waited upon the thronging customers. Oranges, bananas, cocoa nuts, plantains, pine apples, and fruits of which I had never heard or dreamed, mangoes, mammoons, mangabas, goyabus, and all the long list of tropical fruits, were heaped in profusion around.

But what images are these that association is evoking from the dark recesses of memory's store-house?

I seem to see among this motley throng a group with graceful forms and fair faces. By fair, I mean beautiful, not blond. These are intensely brunette, another style of beauty. Indeed, the blood in the cheeks, as seen through the transparent skin, has a tinge that is faintly duskish. But the rich lips have caught their tint from the red rose bud—such lips as are sweetest in a caress, and from which you are most unwilling to part.

The eyes are intensely black, liquid fountains having Lethean power, so that whoever looks into their depths forgets much that men ought always to remember.

I welcome back from a period of forgetfulness these returning images, and present them now as characteristic types of the females of that race and clime.

Under the influence of some pleasing excitement, these were animated, vivacious, sparkling, voluble of sweet, rippling sounds.

But when excitement is wanting, all this animation is said to be wanting also, and languor and repose, are most characteristic.

A combination of these charms I have enumerated, with permanent energy of character, and vivacity, sometimes springs from a union, under temperate skies, of this race with the stirring Anglo-Saxon.

And this combination makes a very, *very* charming individual.

The writer knows whereof he writes.

One day of our stay in Rio was Sunday. Early

in the morning, having donned our best clothes, my brother, a cousin, and myself went on shore for an extended stroll about the city.

We did not waste any time in viewing again what we had already seen, but, passing rapidly into the Palace Square, we turned to the left, moving more slowly when the familiar localities were left behind.

For some time our view was limited, but, as we went forward, suddenly, and without any intimation of what was coming, there was opened to us a wide and magnificent prospect.

Right before us lay the Passeio Publico, the public promenade of the capitol of Brazil, with its beautiful, but strange, trees, shrubs, and flowers. Here nature, prolific beyond description, had been aided by the cultivated taste of man, and money in profusion.

On the right, the hill of Santa Theresa showed a brow wreathed with green tropic trees, and a base girdled with white cottages. Beyond the Passeio Publico, distant summits of mountains were visible, and the crowns of nearer hills, and the towers of public edifices, and, here and there, stretches of water, silvery in the morning calm.

One side of the Passeio Publico comes down to the shore, and at this point there is a wide terrace. Here you walk on pavements of variegated marble, and at the extremities of the terrace, stand little airy, elegant chapels, or shrines.

We pressed forward to this terrace, and, standing within an angle of it, hushed our talk and gazed.

Across the water we beheld the picturesque shores about Jurujuba Bay. Through the entrance to the harbor we looked upon the ocean beyond, and saw, for a small space, the sky and water meeting. To the south, the towering Sugar Loaf challenged our admiration.

In the same direction, but close at hand, the green summit of Gloria Hill rose behind the tall tower of Gloria Church.

Sights so grand and so novel had one effect upon us, if we were untutored. Our tongues were still.

We were soon in motion again, going this time in a direction that led away from the shore, and back towards the suburbs of the city. We saw in many gardens, the orange tree with its green leaves, white flowers, and yellow fruit. It was strange to us to see flower and fruit on the same bough. Tiny humming birds darted about, gay enough in their golden and green feathers.

The air was fragrant with the perfume of the rose, the myrtle, and the citron.

As we went we had frequent glimpses of the tall palms, that in many places grew on the sides and the summits of the hills.

At length we issued from the city. We had passed a church, into which people were going, and my companions wished to return and enter that. I did not care to accompany them, so we separated, and I walked on. I soon got tired of this, and sat down in the shade at the base of a great cliff. Over the face of the cliff there was a yellowish skin of moss, or lichen. The same was on the stones among which I sat, at its base. Sitting there, and looking out upon the heated landscape, I grew desperately sick at heart.

Oh, for power to inhale the balsamic odors of the pine and fir! Oh, for a power to look upon the yellow buttercups and red clover, and the green fields where they bloom!

By and by a slight scratching sound attracted my attention, and brought me back from an imaginary journey a long way North. For a time I could see nothing, nor could I fix the direction of the sound; but at length, looking steadily at an angle of the cliff, I saw a number of little diamond shaped heads thrust out, and in each head was a very brilliant pair of black, bead-like eyes, that scanned me very earnestly. I sat perfectly motionless, and soon the heads were followed by legs, bodies, and tails, until half a dozen, or more little lizards were revealed.

If I made the slightest motion, they at once disappeared, their claws rattling and scratching in the dry, husky moss. But they soon returned, and seemed desirous of making a closer acquaintance. No doubt we should have become very intimate if time had permitted, but I remembered that the boat would land for us at noon, and I bade my sprightly friends good-bye, and left them, I thought, in a very regretful mood.

At the landing I found my companions, and we were soon on board.

Going into the cabin I saw that it was decorated with bunting, and that its inmates were unusually animated. Dinner was over, but some still sat at the table, and among them a fine looking, white haired old gentleman, to whom the captain, when he had beckoned us to him, introduced us, saying:

"My boys, Gov. Kent."

Gov. Kent, Ex-Governor of Maine, was the American Consul at Rio during the Taylor-Fillmore administration. Many of the passengers were his old political friends and supporters. It was the day of their triumph, and, all things considered, they both wished and thought it their duty to *dine* him—and they had dined him.

I have endeavored to present, in the favorable light in which they appeared to me, all things that I saw in and around this tropical city.

But, I remember that a day or two before our departure, I experienced a disagreeable sensation in one of my great toes, and, after some ado about it, there was found inside of the skin, on the underneath part of the toe, a *chigoe* that was about to set up housekeeping, and raise a family.

A chigoe is a kind of a flea, that, in the tropics, gets under the skin and produces other chigoes with remarkable rapidity.

I have been telling about the beauties of the tropics. The affair of the chigoe suggests that there are also annoyances there. Now learn about these annoyances.

Sidney Smith says:

"The bête rouge lays the foundation of a tremendous ulcer. In a moment you are covered with ticks. Chigoes bury themselves in your flesh and hatch a colony of young chigoes in a few hours. They will not live together, but every chigoe sets up a separate ulcer, and has his own private portion of pus. Flies get entry into your mouth, into your eyes, into your nose; you eat flies, drink flies, and breathe flies. Lizards, cockroaches, and snakes get into the bed; ants eat up the books; scorpions sting you on the foot. Everything bites, stings or bruises. Every second of your existence you are wounded by some piece of animal life that nobody has ever seen before, except Swammerdam and Meriam. An insect with eleven legs is swimming in your teacup, and a nondescript of nine wings is struggling in the small beer, or a caterpillar, with several dozen eyes in his belly, is hastening over the bread and butter. All nature is alive, and seems to be gathering her entomological hosts to eat you up, as you are standing, out of your coat, waistcoat, and breeches. Such are the tropics."

CHAPTER XI.

THE EMPIRE OF BRAZIL.—DEPARTURE FROM RIO.

I HAVE read somewhere of a Jesuit in South America, who was desirous of observing the habits of the chigoe, and who, for this purpose, allowed them to effect a lodgement in one of his feet, and extend their operations there, without let or hindrance.

The desired knowledge of the insect's habits was gained, *but the foot was lost.*

Such devotion to science is rare, and happily so.

After the little family in my toe had been broken up, I was careful not to strip off my shoes and stockings and wade on the beach, as I had previously done, when left to take care of the boat at the landing.

I do not wish to leave so interesting a country as Brazil without furnishing some information concerning it, besides the very little derived from personal observation. I shall, therefore, mostly fill up this chapter with such facts and figures on the subject as are least frequently met in print.

When we think of the vast territorial extent, the splendid climate, the inexhaustible magazines of gold and precious stones, the valuable staples, the noble rivers, and fine harbors of Brazil—when we think of all this, and remember, that to Spain, powerful, jealous, avaricious, and greedy of empire, belonged the honor of its discovery, we wonder how Portugal, comparatively weak, though equally greedy of territory, ever obtained a title to it.

The claim of original discovery is put forward, but that is false.

The discovery of a part of this continent by Spain, was, really and actually, a discovery of it all, from Cape Horn to the frozen ocean on the north.

But beside this general, there was also a special discovery.

Pinzon, one of the companions of Columbus, discovered Brazil, in the vicinity of Cape St. Augustine, in January, 1500, and took possession of it for Spain, three months before its accidental discovery by Cabral, the Portugese navigator.

Its possession by Portugal really seems to have been the result of good nature and ignorance, on the part of Spain, and perseverance on the part of her neighbor.

The Portugese had already made some discoveries to the south. These discoveries, the Pope, by the issuing of a Papal bull, had conferred upon

Portugal, and also *all* lands that might be discovered within certain limits in that direction.

After the return of Columbus from his first voyage, Ferdinand desired the Pope to confer upon Spain, in a similar manner, the land that Columbus had discovered, and all that he might discover in the western seas.

It was cheerfully done.

His Holiness also defined a line which should be a boundary line between the field of Portugal, and the field of Spain. It was an imaginary straight line drawn from the North Pole to the South Pole, 100 leagues to the west of the Azores and Cape de Verde Islands. All to the west (*and south also*, if any one can tell where that is,) of this line pertained to Spain.

This arrangement did not suit the Portugese King, and he did not cease to agitate the matter, until, through the good nature of Spain, displayed in the Treaty of Tordesillas, in 1494, the Papal line of demarkation was removed to 370 leagues west of the Cape de Verde Islands.

It was in this way that Spain yielded to Portugal the title to a greater part of the territory now embraced in Brazil, if Portugese should discover it. And they did contrive to maintain Cabral's claim, although it was false.

And now in regard to the part ignorance displayed in the transaction.

Had Spain suspected the richness of Brazil, in metals and gems, it never would have permitted the flag of Portugal to wave there.

But it was suspected by neither of the two countries, and, while one spoiled Mexico and Peru, and the other reaped golden harvests in the East Indies, Brazil had no repute, and was neglected.

It was not until toward the middle of the eighteenth century that the mineral resources of the country were properly appreciated.

The total area of Brazil is estimated at 2,760,000 square miles.

This is more than two-thirds the whole extent of Europe, and exceeds the whole territory of the United States. It lies on both sides of the line, extending on the south into the temperate zone.

Probably no country in the world produces so great a variety of animal and vegetable life.

I will dispose of this part of the subject by quoting a paragraph from Lieut. Herndon. He says of Brazil on the Amazon:

"This is the country of rice, of sarsaparilla, of india rubber, balsam copaiba, gum copal, animal and vegetable wax, cocoa, Brazilian nutmegs, Tonka beans, ginger, black pepper, arrowroot, tapioca, annatto, indigo, sapacaia, and Brazil nuts, dyes of the gayest colors, drugs of rare virtue, variegated cabinet woods of the finest grain, and susceptible of the highest polish.

"The forests are filled with game, and the rivers stocked with turtle and fish. Here dwell the anta, or the wild cow, the peixe boi, or fish ox, the sloth, the ant-eater, the beautiful black tiger, the mysterious electric eel, the boa-constrictor, the anaconda, the deadly coral snake, the voracious alligator, monkeys in endless variety, birds of the most brilliant plumage, and insects of the strangest forms and gayest colors."—*Lieut. Herndon's Report, page* 369.

Cotton and tobacco are native plants. Some suppose the sugar cane to have been indigenous, also, while others trace it, or pretend to trace it, back to the old world.

The coffee tree is not a native. The first one that took root in Brazilian soil, was planted at Rio Janeiro, in 1754.

There is displayed in the arms of the Empire, branches adorned with leaves and flowers. These, I was told, represented branches of the coffee tree, and this fact is significant.

And as the arms of the Empire are emblazoned upon its flag, the green leaves and snowy flowers of the coffee tree are seen wherever the flag flies.

Well may the Brazilians do honor to the coffee plant, for it is a source of incalculable wealth to the nation.

Brazil produces gold, diamonds, the ruby, the opal, the topaz, and the sapphire—produces them in abundance. But the search for them has not generally been skilfully conducted, nor have the conveniences for mining been sufficient to produce great results.

Therefore when the net gains of the nation from precious metals and precious stones, are compared with its net gains from even its coffee crop alone, the comparison is all in favor of agriculture.

And this would still be the case, were the greatest skill, and the most perfect apparatus, and the greatest amount of labor, applied to the discovery and collection of gold and diamonds. Agricultural products are, of all products, and everywhere, the greatest sources of wealth.

From the Sugar Loaf, at the entrance of the bay, to the anchorage, is about four miles. The bay here is two miles wide. From the city to the head of the bay is fourteen miles, or eighteen from the entrance. The greatest width at any point is twelve miles. It is one of the best, and most secure harbors in the world, as well as one of the most beautiful and most easy of access. The armed ships of all the great maritime powers are always to be found here. Great quantities of powder are burnt in saluting. There was a roar of cannon nearly all the time.

The Palace of San Christovao, the residence of the Emperor, has a very beautiful and romantic location, a few miles to the west of the city.

The supply of water, which is abundant and of an excellent quality, comes by an aqueduct from Corcovado, " the broken backed," a mountain three or four miles to the south-west.

We lay only a little distance from the Island and Fortress of Villegagnon. You will probably know, or guess, that that is a French name. The man whose name it bears was Nicholas Durand de Villegagnon. Fidelity in this man would have given Brazil to Frenchmen and Protestantism. His treachery gave it to Portugal and Romanism.

An addition of one was made to our ship's company at Rio. The self-destruction of the old steward had caused a vacancy in the culinary department, and this additional man was shipped to fill it. Being especially a cook, however, he was stationed in the galley, and not the pantry. Though a negro, and rather a black one, his personal appearance was quite prepossessing. He was small in stature, finely proportioned, and bore always a very pleasing expression upon his countenance. According to his story, his home was in Baltimore. He had come from that city to Rio in a barque. I do not remember why he left her. He was rather destitute, and before entering upon his duties, desired a month's advance pay, and liberty to go on shore and make some purchases. To provide against desertion on his part, my brother was sent with him.

They proceeded to a ship chandler's, and the new cook made purchases as follows:

    Item, A glass of gin.
      "   A bar of soap.
      "   A glass of gin.
      "   Half a dozen needles.
      "   A glass of gin.
      "   Half a pound of linen thread.
      "   A glass of gin.

At this stage of the proceedings my brother interfered in such a decided manner, that gin was omitted until the purchases were all made. Then the worthy African remarked that in Baltimore, where he was brought up, when a man had bought a bill of goods of a merchant, the merchant generally treated. The hint was sufficient.

So much *cause* (five glasses), could not help producing some effect. The effect was in direct proportion, it being six hours of boisterous drunkenness, and seventy-two hours of consequent sickness.

Nov. 16th, in the morning, we hove the anchor up, and departed from Rio. It was a regulation of the port that all foreign vessels going out should set their ensigns at the fore, and give a password to the guard at the Castle of Santa Cruz. A day or two before, an English brig, in starting, hoisted her colors as usual at the main peak.

She had not fanned along far with the light breeze, before bang, went a gun from Villegagnon. No notice was taken of it. Two more were fired with the same effect, or, rather, want of effect. Probably the disposition to fire a shot was not wanting in the fortress, but it was not gratified, for some reason or other. After the third discharge, a boat pulled off and boarded the brig, and her flag was then transferred to the foremast head.

We were able to both comply with, and to violate the regulation. We had two ensigns. One was displayed at the fore, and the other took its accustomed place at the spanker gaff.

The password given us was, when translated into English, "The Brazilians are brave."

By the way, the opinion then generally entertained by foreigners was that the Brazilians were *not* brave. They must modify that opinion now, for they certainly are proving themselves brave in their sanguinary war with Paraguay.

Our password was written out upon a piece of paper, and when we were abreast the Castle, the captain roared it out through his trumpet, giving it such accents as suited his fancy. The guard allowed it was all right, and waved us along.

Our demeanor and language had been very respectful, both when going in by, and when coming out by the Castle of Santa Cruz. The power of the garrison to resent an insult was very apparent; and men in that condition often feel insulted when they would not otherwise.

But "familiarity breeds contempt." Veteran shipmasters in the Rio trade have a great contempt for all these customs.

Ten years after our departure from the harbor of Rio, my brother entered it again as mate of a barque. In passing Santa Cruz, he said, the same soldier (for anything he knew to the contrary), using the same words, and having the same execrable accent, hailed—

"What sheep is that?"

"Go to the devil," replied the captain.

My brother was astonished and alarmed. But the soldier was unruffled.

"Vare well," said he. "Where you from?"

"And shake yourself," answered the captain, continuing his inelegant quotation.

"Vare well. Where you bound?"

"You blackguard," responded the captain in conclusion.

"Vare well," (polite wave of the hand,) "I tank you, sar."

The soldier was repeating, parrot fashion, what he had been taught. He did not understand a single word of English, and of this the captain was well aware.

I said that when my father had given the password, the sentinel on the rampart admitted its correctness, and waved us along.

But the wind failing just then, we were quite unable to comply. Sea after sea threw us in, until I could have tossed a stone into the grinning muzzles of the guns. It seemed as if we must anchor, or go ashore. But it did not come to that. There was a powerful undertow that impelled us off as much as the sea urged us on.

At length an air of wind came to our relief. The sails left off threshing the masts, and swelling out, steadied the ship and urged her forward.

The Castle receded; the wide muzzles of the guns grew more and more diminutive, and finally disappeared.

The land was like a dark cloud when night closed around us, and out of the darkness it came never again to greet our eyes.

CHAPTER XII

TROPICAL BIRDS AND FISHES—THE "DOCTOR."

RIO JANEIRO lies in 22° 54' south latitude, and a few hours sail carries us beyond the tropic of Capricorn.

Before leaving the torrid zone behind entirely, I will hastily describe some of the birds and fishes that we encountered in crossing it.

Some of these are peculiar to the region, while others are confined to no particular locality.

The whale is an inhabitant of nearly all parts of all seas.

It is not necessary that I should take time to describe an animal so often, and so minutely described; but, inasmuch as I asked the young people in a former chapter, whether the whale was a fish, or not, I will say a few words in that direction.

The whale is *not* properly a fish. It breathes pure air. A fish breathes air only as it exists in water. The whale is warm-blooded. A fish is cold-blooded. The whale brings forth its young alive and suckles them with true milk. It is classed by naturalists with mammals, and considered such as much as the horse or the elephant.

The tropic bird is, as its name would imply, peculiar to that region. In size it is somewhat larger than the common pigeon. Its color is white, variegated by occasional black places upon the back, and upon the ends of the larger feathers of the wings. Its bill, legs and feet are red, the latter exceedingly so.

The most striking thing about it, however, is its tail, which consists of two very long, straight, and narrow feathers, just alike in all respects.

When it poised itself far up overhead, as it often did, it was not altogether unlike a musical note written on the blue sky.

The booby, which is encountered here, and for some distance beyond the tropics in each direction, is in some respects a most remarkable bird. Its invincible stupidity gained for it its undesirable name. No "fresh salt" to throw on the tail is necessary to effect its capture. Whether you meet it on the rocks on land, or climb to it on the spars of a ship at sea, it is not alarmed at your approach, and you may kick it in the one case, and cuff it in the other, but all in vain to drive it. It will stand its grounds while life and strength remain. This peculiarity of the booby conduces to the benefit of man. It is a law of nature, or a provision of Providence in nature that *there*, (whether it is comprehensible or incomprehensible to him,) "all things shall work together for good" to man.

Men, compelled by cruel circumstances to navigate the wide ocean in frail boats, and destitute of water and provisions, have been saved from death, or from an alternative worse than death—eating each other—by this wonderful tameness of the booby. Lieutenant Bligh and his companions, set adrift in mid ocean by the mutineers of the Bounty, say that when they were in a most deplorable state, they caught some boobies that flew very near to them. These they killed and gave their blood to those who were most distressed for want of food, while the bodies with the *entrails, beak and feet*, they divided among the others.

This occurred more than once; and said Lieutenant Bligh, "Providence seemed to be relieving our wants in an extraordinary manner."

This case of the Lieutenant and his companions has often been paralleled in the records of the sea, and more than paralleled.

The color of the booby is a dull brown. In length it is about two and a half feet. Its bill is long and sharp at the extremity, and large where it is joined to the head.

I remember very distinctly the first booby I saw. The sun had gone down and it was growing duskish when some one discovered a dark object aloft on one of the spars. The mate, who was on deck, at once declared it to be a booby, and sent one of the boys aloft to catch it. There was a short struggle when the boy reached it, and seized it by the legs. The booby protested by voice, and by deed against capture, but was obliged to yield to superior force. As an evidence of his unwillingness to be taken, however, he inflicted two or three severe wounds upon the boy's hands. But at no time did it manifest a disposition to fly away.

The ship's company generally paid their respects to it, and then it was thrown into the air. Instead of flying away as one would suppose, it alighted again aloft, where it was permitted to spend the night in peace.

Unlike human boobies, who do not display much ability in any direction, this feathered booby is an industrious and dexterous fisherman, and always contrives to provide well for himself and family.

The frigate bird, a large black-looking bird, with a forked tail and an immense spread of wings, is generally found in the haunts of the booby.

They are called frigate birds, because like men-of-war, they spread a broad clue and are very swift in flight. The resemblence ends there, however, for the acts of the frigate bird are altogether unjustifiable. He victimizes the poor booby. He lies in wait for him when he is returning from his fishing excursions, and falls aboard of him, and bumps him and thumps him with his wings, and pecks him with his bill, until he disgorges his hard-earned dinner, which the frigate bird, quitting him, catches in its descent.

Whether the booby disgorges voluntarily to save a whole skin, or whether it is an involuntary act resulting from the shocks he receives, we shall never know certainly until our means of communicating with animals is improved.

Is not this play of frigate bird and booby often enacted by men in communities?

The stormy petrel, or mother Cary's chicken, to which I have already alluded as an object of superstition to the sailor, is not peculiar to any region, but a true cosmopolitan. These birds are in size between a sparrow and a robin. In their flights they resemble martins. Their backs are brown, bellies white, tails short and forked, and wings long and pointed.

Their beaks bend suddenly at the tips, making a short, sharp hook.

They keep at sea generally, but nevertheless go to land sometimes.

They frequent one of the Western Islands. The people kill great numbers of them for their oil. So very fat are they that, it it said, the Islanders just draw a wick through their bodies, and it becomes so saturated with liquid fat as to form a lamp without anything else. The same thing is said to be done at Faroe Islands, away up between Scotland and Ireland. These little birds fly about ships, coming fearlessly close aboard. Their object is the one great object of all living creatures, viz: to procure food. Much is thrown overboard from a ship each day that they can appropriate in that way,

They seem to enjoy a gale of wind, and clamber around among the waves in a way that indicates great happiness. Sometimes they enter a wave and are hid from view for a little while.

It is very natural to pass from a consideration of birds to a consideration of fishes by the way of the flying-fish, which partakes of the nature of both.

The flying-fish and the flying-squirrel are anomalies in nature.

They might serve as steps to let us down to mermen and mermaidens in the water, and Count Castlenau's men with tails on the land, if ever it should prove that there were such creatures. I suppose these chimeras seem no more impossible to us than winged-fish and flying-squirrels have seemed, and do seem to many minds. Such incredulity is amusingly expressed in Cooper's Pathfinder, where the mariner, Cap. with his flying-*fish*, and the Pathfinder with his flying-*squirrel*, more than suspect each other of wholesale deception.

The flying-fish, is shaped much like other fish, and is in length, all the way from five to twenty inches. It has a blue and mottled back like the mackerel, and a white belly. The membranaceous pectoral fins, the wings of the flying-fish, are about half the length of the body. They are attached to the shoulders of the fish by uncommonly strong muscles. The flight of this fish is several hundred feet. There is a difference of opinion among naturalists as to whether these pectoral fins are used as parachutes or wings.

When cooked, the flying-fish is very attractive food.

The motive of this fish in flying through the air, is not always the same. Sometimes it is to escape from other fishes that prey upon them, and sometimes it must certainly be for the enjoyment of the thing.

One sight awakens peculiar emotion. It is to see the flying-fish and the mother Cary's chicken exchanging elements. The fish rising and cleaving the air, and the bird disappearing in the slanting side of a wave like a swallow entering his hole in a bank.

Flying-fish frequently fly on board of vessels, not purposely, but accidentally, in their endeavors to escape from the jaws of some pursuing enemy. They have many enemies, and it was no rare thing to witness their pursuit and destruction by the coryphene, (commonly called the dolphin,) and the albacore.

A variety of the flying-fish is said to be found sometimes in the Mediterranean with four wings behind the gills, instead of two. Their bodies are of a bright violet color. They are seen but rarely.

The coryphene is more widely known as the *dolphin*, while the true dolphin is called a porpoise.

The head of the coryphene is short and like that of the cat-fish, without the cat-fish's malignant expression; the body is deep and thin. The dorsal fin extends from the back of the head to the tail. The tail is prodigiously forked. These fish vary in length from two to five feet. They display a variety of colors; on the back and sides a bluish green with reflections of azure and gold, and beneath that a yellow with bright blue tints. Their fins are also brilliantly colored.

They are always seen in the tropics, swimming

in company with vessels. They are frequently taken, sometimes upon a hook, and sometimes with the grains.

The flesh of the coryphene is generally eaten, though it has sometimes been found poisonous.

A test of its wholesomeness is to put a piece of silver with it when it is cooked; if the silver is not tarnished it is all right.

The true dolphin and the porpoise differ but little. The dolphin's jaws are lengthened out into a long beak, not unlike that of a bird. The dolphin keeps in blue water; the porpoise is more a shoal water animal.

Both belong to the order of cataceous mammals as well as the whale, and are therefore not properly fishes.

But all this is rather irrelevant, and with a few more words I will change the subject. To have a just conception of these birds, and fishes—particularly the fishes—one must see them living and moving in their native elements. Death robs them of many of their peculiar attractions.

No method of preservation, however excellent, unless life is involved in it, can preserve in these fishes that brilliancy of color that varies with every emotion. And could life be preserved, there would still be something wanting. Like gems that require the proper setting to bring out all their beauties, the coryphene, the labacore and the bonito, require to be set in a blue sea and under a vertical sun, to bring out all their beauties.

And it is also very hard for any one, without seeing it, to get a just conception of that deep water, near the surface of which these fishes swim.

In a calm, one can look far down into its blue depths. It seems filled with light. Under the counters of the ship the little rudder fish dart in and out. Coryphenes, sometimes singly, sometimes in pairs, and sometimes half a dozen together, swim slowly into view. Their deliberate motions show you, one by one, all the colors of the rainbow. Alarm them, and their quicker motions blend all those colors into one. The eye beholds, as it were, continuous explosions of brilliant colors under the surface of the water.

Such exhibitions, constantly occurring, break the monotony of long sea voyages, and render what might otherwise be tiresome, interesting and instructive.

Our black cook, when sober, we found, was not at all the same man that he was when drunk. Under the first influences of five glasses of gin his volubility was amazing. When sober he hardly ever spoke except to answer a question.

Then, though very respectful in his tone, he used monosyllables only, unless more words were absolutely necessary. He was also very neat and very industrious. He had the habits of the bee, but did not hum and buzz like that model insect.

I have introduced this colored individual, not because *color* is the fashion now-a-days, but because where others were faithless, he alone was faithful.

His feet hardly left the deck from the time he brought the five glasses of gin over the rail at Rio, until at Battery Wharf in Boston, he placed upon the table the last dinner we ate on Board. His only failing was a desire to illustrate the old saying, "when rum (gin in this case) is in, wit is out;" but opportunities for doing this did not often occur.

He had quite an agreeable surprise when we were a few days out from Rio.

A passenger, one of those individuals who manifest an intense interest in the affairs of others, and who are unhappy if any body is near them whose history they do not know, said to him:

"Doctor, were you ever a slave?",

(A black cook is always dubbed Doctor, on ship board.)

"Yes," answered the Doctor.

"Did you run away?"

"No."

"Then you are lawfully free, hey?"

"Yes."

A pause, and then from the passenger.

"Have you your free papers about you?"

"No.'

Another pause, and then.

"Where are they?"

"I loss dem in Rio," the Doctor said this with a sigh of regret.

At this, a sailor, who was within earshot, turned quickly around, and having scanned the Doctor's person, asked,

"What is your name?"

"Henry Brown."

"What," said the sailor, "will you give me to get your papers again?"

"It's no use to talk," answered the cook, mournfully shaking his head, "it's gone."

"You just wait a minute," said the man, diving down into the forecastle. When he returned, he had a document in his hand, which he handed the Doctor, saying,

"Did you ever see that before?"

The little black man was excited.

"Where you get dis?" he said.

"Looks natural, does it?"

"How you come by dis, I say?"

The man explained. A soldier in the streets of Rio offered to sell it to him, and when he would not buy, gave it to him.

In such a way, after it had been lost, came

Henry Brown's certificate of freedom back to him again. The passenger had one more question, and he put it.

"Ain't you glad you've got it again," he asked.

CHAPTER XIII.

BIRD CATCHING.—FISHING.—ENTER THE PACIFIC.

FRIDAY, December 7, we were in south latitude 47° 40'. Here we experienced a very heavy gale from the south-west. For twenty-four hours the ship was hove to under the main spencer, a small, stout, fore and aft sail on the mainmast.

We had seen nothing like it before—no wind so fierce, and no waves so high. Down between the seas it was calm and comparatively still, but when the ship was lifted up to their summits, the mingled roar of wind and waves was appalling to ears unaccustomed to it. The ship behaved admirably, proving herself an excellent sea boat. She was quite crank, and on this account lay to better. The wind upon her naked spars and rigging was alone sufficient to press her lee gunwale into the water, and prevent her from rolling to windward.

Toward noon the gale abated some. The close reefed topsail, reefed foresail, and foretopmast staysail were set, and the ship began to forge ahead slowly.

We had exchanged the tropic bird for the albatross; but the stormy petrels still gave us the pleasure of their company, and had introduced to us in addition, the giant petrel, the cape pigeon, and other members of the petrel family, their kindred.

By the way, *petrel* is said to be derived from the diminutive of Peter. The stormy petrel, with outstretched, but motionless wings, runs upon the surface of the water, and this habit, by its resemblance to the well known attempt of Peter on Lake Gennesaret, fastened upon them and their species, among Christians, the scriptural name they bear.

Many Southern Atlantic birds were about us. At one time an albatross would be nearest. Round about us he would hover, on his ample wings, now darting in advance, and now settling in our wake astern. Then he would poise himself right above us, and make a deliberate survey of the quarter deck, and then whirl away to leeward. At another time some member of the petrel family would be the inspector. Often they would all come together, and the air would seem alive with their swift wings. Whatever was thrown overboard they darted down upon with the greatest rapidity.

Their voracity suggested to us (or revived our knowledge of the fact), that they might be captured by baiting a hook and trolling it astern. Accordingly a line was brought up, prepared, and then veered away.

Immediately the bait, a piece of pork, caught the eye of a hungry albatross. A few sweeps of his broad wings was sufficient to place him within reach of it; and then, partly alighting, and partly hovering, he thrust forward his neck and seized the pork with his bill.

True to its office, the barbed steel pierced through, and the free bird of the ocean was a captive. When drawn on board, he was released as gently as possible from the hook, and placed upon the deck. Such birds are unable to rise and fly from a ship's deck, therefore no one stood near enough to him to render him uneasy. He was awed not one whit by the presence of his captors. His large round eye was at once mild and dauntless. His whole bearing was kingly and graceful.

The albatross is the largest sea bird known. It has a pale yellow bill, a gray head, and a white body, marked on the back by a few black bands.

The largest one of which I have seen any record, was shot off the Cape of Good Hope. It measured seventeen and a half feet from tip to tip of the wings.

The line having been veered out a second time, was soon hauled in again with a new specimen at the end of it. This was a bird smaller than the albatross, but of the same shape. It was white upon the breast and forward part of the neck, and otherwise of a dark brown color. A child of the ocean it undeniably was, yet when it had been placed for a short time upon the deck it showed unmistakable signs of sea-sickness. The bird actually vomited. Doubtless it was the motion of the ship, in which it was compelled to participate, that caused it to be so painfully afflicted.

Subsequently a second and third albatross were caught. The latter was very large and powerful. As soon as he was hooked, he thrust his broad wings down edgewise into the water, determined to resist to the utmost all attempts to draw him on board. Had not the line been new and strong, and the hook of good steel, he would have escaped.

But the tackling was all firm, and the hook had a strong hold upon him. Willing hands manned the line, and slowly, foot by foot, the brave bird was drawn toward the ship. The whole surface of his wings, many square feet, *all alive*, resisted powerfully, and then, too, the ship was moving along at the rate of three or four miles an hour.

Suddenly the resistance of the bird ceased; his wings rose upward out of the water, and he was easily drawn over the remaining distance to the ship. He was dead. His neck, unable to bear the unaccustomed and tremendous strain, broke. There was but one feeling in reference to this bird among his captors, and that was genuine respect for him. His love of the freedom wherein he was born, his determined hostility to captivity, his consistent and manly resistance even unto death, struck a sympathetic cord in all our breasts.

He measured ten feet from the tip of one wing to the tip of the other. His bill was preserved by my brother, and now ornaments a shelf in the Museum of a New Hampshire Academy.

With the capture of this bird our fishing ended for that time. The birds on deck were picked up, tossed into the air, and told to look out for themselves.

This they were glad to do, and they manifested their joy in eccentric flights.

On the 12th we were becalmed, about a hundred miles to the westward of the Falkland Islands. A discussion arose in regard to the depth of the water, and to decide it, the order was given to pass along the lead and line. Everything was soon in readiness and the lead thrown over. Down it went, exciting some wonder, probably, among the inhabitants of the deep, as to what it was, whence it came, whither it was going, and why it had such a long tail. What inquiries it did raise down in the watery realm beneath us, we could not know, and indeed did not care. We sent it to seek the bottom, and like a faithful servant it found it, sixty-two fathoms down under us. One passenger, who was an old mariner, proposed that it be hauled up and *armed*, and then sent down a second time to ascertain the character of the bottom it had discovered. Another passenger, who was *not* a mariner, inquired whether it would be armed with firearms, or steel. For his part he thought powder would be of little or no service under water.

Well, the lead was armed—not with pistol or dirk-knife, but with *bar soap*, stuck into a cavity in its bottom, and sent down again. When it was hauled up the soap was coated with dark gray sand.

Then it was proposed to fish. Many laughed, and were skeptical in regard to the existence here of fish that swim near the bottom.

The idea of fishing prevailed, however. One brought hooks and attached them, another visited the harness-cask and abstracted a piece of pork, and a third hurried for a knife to cut bait with. When all things were ready, the lead was cast over. As soon as it was down one individual took hold of the line, drew it up until he judged the baits to be the requisite distance from the bottom, and then impatiently awaited a bite. He waited as vainly as impatiently. He put in practice the arts of the wary fisherman. He gently drew the line up a short distance, and as gently lowered it down again. This was intended to make a dazzling display of the baits before the eyes of the fishes. That failing, he suddenly drew up several feet of the line, saying, by this act, to any fish that might be dallying with the bait, as the auctioneer says to the human fish about his bait, "*going, going.*" All a hoax. This everlasting "going—going," is only to force a bite. When "*gone*" is cried the nominal biter is always bitten.

His arts all failing, the first fisherman, discouraged, resigned the line to another. The same story over again. This second man began hopefully, continued impatiently, and, by-and-by, gave up the line willingly. The same result followed trials by a third man and a fourth man, and then the line was fastened to a pin, and left to its own reflection—if lines ever do reflect.

In about one hour there were signs of wind abroad, and the order was given to haul in the line. A man laid hold of it and hauled in. When he had about half accomplished his task, he stopped, held the line off from the side, struck an attitude of intense attention, and pretty soon declared that he believed he had a fish.

Others proposed to hold the line, and see what impression they would get, but to this the man would not consent, and himself pulled away as if for dear life.

All eyes were now in requisition, and if inanimate matter could blush, the water would certainly have done so.

Fathom after fathom of line came swiftly up, and lay dripping upon the deck.

"There he is!"

"There's a fish!"

"Well, I declare!"

Such exclamations were frequent when the lead appeared, and below it a dull whitish substance, writhing about in the water.

It was a dog-fish, (*Squalus Acanthias*.)

The signs of a breeze apparent, when the line was hauled up, proved to be genuine indications.

A brisk wind sprung up from the north-west. Ths sails were trimmed, and our course laid for Cape Horn. Gradually the wind increased. The log-book shows first one knot (or one mile per hour), then two, then three, four, six, seven, eight, ten and eleven.

Much satisfaction was manifested by all on board, and many sanguine spirits rubbed their hands constantly and walked about exclaiming:

"What a glorious wind! We shall double the Cape in the twinkling of an eye!"

As the long day was drawing to a close, the rare cry of "land ho!" was heard aloft. I climbed up the fore-rigging, and as my head rose above the fore-yard, I saw, far away on the starboard bow a group of dark objects nestled down on the turbulent water. It was the northern end of Staten Land, and fifty miles or more distant from us. Staten Land is a small island, separated from Tierra del Fuego by the straits of Le Maire. At its southern extremity the southern continent of America curves to the eastward. Staten Land seems like a piece smitten off from that extremity.

It was not dark at that season of the year, where we were, until after nine o'clock, and then it could not be called dark; it was only a deep twilight.

At two o'clock in the morning, the low, disconnected objects I had seen from the fore-yard, had grown to one tall headland. It was Cape St. John, the north-eastern extremity of Staten Land, and bore from us then south-south-west distant about eighteen miles. At noon it was away on the northern board.

The atmosphere was far from being clear, and, even when nearest to it, the glass gave no better view of the land than the naked eye. I looked at it with interest, but had not the keen relish for it that I had for Fernando Noronha. The charm that held me then was broken. A vast number of birds were flying between us and the shore, but they were too distant to distinguish peculiarities.

"We shall round the Cape in a twinkling," had been a hundred times said. Another instance of man's fallibility. At noon the wind began to lessen. At two P. M., it was calm, and a fine rain falling. At three, a puff struck us from the south, and at four, it blew a gale from that direction, accompanied by hail and sleet. The ship was put under close reefed topsails and came up southeast by south on the starboard tack.

The great disappointment of all was somewhat softened by the fine run of the previous day. In the twenty-four hours we had sailed over two hundred miles. .

Six days succeeded before we were fairly into the Pacific. The wind was ahead all the time, but never, after the first day, did it blow very hard. The sea was regular and never high. I do not find the temperature anywhere noted, but you can judge about what midsummer weather is in latitude 57°.

The sky was much overcast. A sombre, gray mantle lined the firmament, and the sun was able to exhibit himself but rarely. We went south as far as the fifty-eighth parallel of latitude.

Cape Horn is a perversion of Cape *Hoorn*. Shouten, a Dutch navigator, in 1616, christened this bleak, inhospitable, tail-end of the Americas, *Cape Hoorn*, after his native town in Holland.

Cape Horn is a sort of focus, the point of convergence of thousands of courses.

It was not strange therefore to see vessels here, although we had seen them but rarely before. There were in sight at one time two ships, one barque and a brig.

December 22, we took a fine breeze from the eastward. We were then well into the Pacific Ocean, and our backs fairly turned upon the gray sombre region of the far south. As a horseman, who has been carefully picking his way along a rough and insecure path, guiding his beast with nerved arms and wary eye, gives him the rein on entering a smooth and level road and gallops onward with a joyous and secure feeling, so we relaxed at once from our Cape Horn watchfulness and preparation, and with eager alacrity send royal yards aloft.

The morning of Christmas was calm. Several vessels were in sight. At five o'clock a boat boarded us from the ship Harriet Rockwell, of Boston. ninety-seven days out from Boston, bound to San Francisco, and having on board ninety-eight passengers.

When ships long out meet at sea, and it is convenient to visit from one to the other, it is an honor to humanity to see in what a warm and hospitable manner the visitors are received. They are taken by the hand eagerly and welcomed to the best that the ship can afford. The cold dignity of the shore, and its distant politeness are not known. And why should the precious time be wasted in ceremonies? Mankind are eminently social. Few were ever intended for hermits. But a ship while at sea is in a certain sense a hermitage. Her mariners, shut out from the rest of the world, and meeting with but little material from which to make talk, by-and-by lose their relish for conversation with each other. At such a time a new man is a God-send, in a practical sense, and it is also the part of self-interest as well as of humanity to welcome him warmly.

At noon a breeze sprang up from the northwest. While lying with the main topsail to the mast for the Harriet Rockwell to come up, the brig Oriental, of Machias, Me., passed us. When their ship was abeam of us, the Rockwellians got into their boat and departed. Our sails were then filled, and we all proceeded on together.

CHAPTER XLV.

A TRIAL OF SPEED—VALPARAISO—THE NORTH STAR—A BLACK EYE—ARRIVAL AT SAN FRANCISCO.

AT the close of the last chapter we were standing in on a wind towards the western coast of Patagonia, in company with the ship Harriet Rockwell and the brig Oriental.

They soon tacked to the westward and by-and-by, we followed their example, but not until they were out of sight. In the night the wind hauled to the south-west, and increased to a gale. We wore ship to the north and reduced our canvass until only the close reefed main topsail, reefed foresail, fore-topmast staysail, and main spencer remained.

At daylight a barque was just visible on the weather quarter, and a brig, the Oriental about six miles astern. It was soon evident that both were gaining upon us. At eight o'clock the barque was abeam, and the brig only a mile astern and right in our wake. The brig was making the water fly finely; great torrents going over her foreyard.

It was rather too mortifying to be outsailed in

that manner, and soon the order came to make sail. The close reefed fore and mizzen topsails, reefed mainsail, jib, main-topmast staysail, and spanker were set. The wind was abeam, and the ship ran in the trough of the sea. How she did go when the extra sail was set! I remember how an old sailor expressed it. He was cuddled up under the break of the poop, to windward, chewing his quid, and complacently spitting great volumes of juice out upon the deck to be quickly swept away by the torrents of water that flew over the rail.

Another tar, having watched his chance so as to escape a wetting, darted from the shelter of the forward house, and joined him. As he crouched by his side, he said:

"The old craft is doing her duty."

"Yes," was the reply, "*she is getting up and naturally howling.*"

At dinner time it was necessary for one to hold himself to the table, and his plate upon it. The dishes leaped up bodily out of the racks. One butter plate, having been thrown upon the deck, canted up on its edge, rolled quite around the table, and then darted through an open door into a stateroom, where it came down, right side up, in a corner. The "monkey," an earthen vessel to hold water, suspended from a beam above the table, carried on riotously, sometimes swinging with long swings fore and aft, sometimes jumping up and down with short spasmodic jumps, and sometimes whirling swiftly around like a top.

On deck one was more uncomfortable than below. The water was no respecter of persons. As many seas came over the weather quarter as over the weather bow.

One wave appalled me. I was standing by the main rigging, and holding on with one hand. Suddenly a shade fell upon the deck. I looked quickly up, and saw just to windward, only a few yards off, a great blue wave, a perpendicular wall of water, towering up higher than our topsail yards. It seemed to totter, and I expected to see the whole overhanging mass tumble upon our deck. Instinctively I tightened my hold upon the rigging. My heart seemed to leap into my mouth. But quickly I felt the ship ascending, steadily and swiftly, and the next moment the dreaded wave, partly fallen down, was beneath us. It is wonderful how even the most misshapen stick of wood will take care of itself in the roughest sea. When one would expect to see it submerged, or hurled end over end, it will rise and fall as gently as if careful hands controlled it. A good ship, skillfully managed, will bid defiance to almost anything short of miraculous power.

We now far outstripped our companions. At noon they had dropped back to their old relative position in the morning. Three hours afterwards they were both out of sight, astern. Having "done enough for glory," we shortened sail.

On the second day of January, 1850, the chains were shackled to the anchors, and other preparations made for a short sojourn at Valparaiso, Chili.

At ten o'clock on the night of the fourth the ship was hove to to wait for daylight. At four o'clock in the morning we filled away and made all sail.

Before the sun rose the Andes were visible, their snowy summits bathed in light. In about an hour the coast line came to view. At noon the light-house on the Point of Angels was plainly to be seen. The wind freshened and there were occasionally violent squalls. The light sails were therefore furled, and we ran in under the three topsails and jib. At half past two we rounded the Point of Angels, which forms the western part of the harbor, and saw suddenly, right before us, the city and the shipping.

The bay, or harbor, of Valparaiso makes in to the south, and is semicircular in form. It is commodious, and well protected from all winds except the north. The city rises round the bay like an amphitheatre. In its rear are high hills having a dry and desolate aspect.

Valparaiso lies in 31° south latitude. The fruits of the middle States of this country are produced there. I had the pleasure of again seeing apples, and tasting them, and this *was* a pleasure, although on account of the season they were old. This part of Chili produces an excellent quality of wheat, of which large quantities are exported.

Ever since the country achieved its independence, Valparaiso has been growing in importance, and is now the second city on the Pacific coast.

While we were lying there, a street fight occurred between the police force and about two hundred English and American men-of-warsmen, who, on this occasion, made common cause.

The tumult was audible on board the vessels in the harbor, and with the glass I could distinguish the brickbats and stones as they flew through the air. One policeman was killed and others badly hurt. There was great excitement in consequence of this, and it had not subsided when we left.

Along shore to the north two or three miles was the place where Com. Porter fought the Essex so gallantly in the last war with England—a fight in which Admiral Farragut, the great naval hero of our civil war, participated as midshipman.

Point of Angels is noted for the fierce squalls that leap down from it, and tear along the surface of the water. It was while hugging this point in order to pass to windward of the English frigate outside, that a squall carried away the Essex's main topmast, and left her at the mercy of her enemies.

Jan. 11th, at noon, we got under way, and stood off to sea from Valparaiso. Before night everything was snug—the anchors stowed and the chains unbent and put below. We had on board six new passengers, Frenchmen.

For twenty-five days we ran off before the south-east trade wind, sighting on the fourteenth of the month the Island of Ambrose. St. Felix and Ambrose are two small, unimportant islands lying near the tropic of Capricorn, in 80° west longitude. All the time the weather was exceedingly pleasant. It was seized upon as a favorable opportunity to set up the rigging and refit the ship in other respects.

Balboa was the first European who beheld the Pacific ocean. In 1513, standing on the mountain of the isthmus, his astonished eyes saw it stretching away placid and bright in the sun's rays. Descending to the shore he bathed in it, and, naming it the Great South Sea, took posession of it on behalf of the King of Spain. Such a proceeding seems to us very presumptuous. It was presumptuous.

It was not, however, until 1520 that a European navigated the new ocean. In that year Magellan, passing through the straits that now bear his name, sailed for three months and twenty days upon it, and during the whole time no storm ruffled its surface.

On this account he gave it the appropriate name of Pacific ocean, a name which all the subsequent navigators unite with him in declaring descriptive of it.

When we had crossed the Equinoctial line again the passengers began to talk of the North Star. There seemed to be a universal and intense desire to behold it. Nightly, sharp eyes skirted the sky along the northern board, and when at length the well-known star did appear, it was hailed with shouts of joy. It had set behind us in the Atlantic —it rose before us in the Pacific.

Faithful star, how it carried us back in imagination to our far off homes! Over them it had watched all our lives, and over them we were confident it was watching then.

The Frenchmen whom we had taken on board at Valparaiso ran over with national characteristics. They were remarkably gay, talkative, and polite. One of them was a bit of a conjurer. He swallowed pistol bullets, and afterwards extracted them from his ears, eyes and nose—changed coppers to half dollars—drew fathom after fathom of twine from his nose—all to the great edification and amusement of his stiffer fingered fellow-passengers.

One of his tricks (not a slight-of-hand one, however,) came near costing him a threshing The passengers generally were sunning themselves upon the deck, when he came among them with a novel contrivance in his hand. It was one of those round, wooden match boxes, which are so common with the cover fastened on and two quills, one long and one short inserted into the sides of it. Between the quills, one of which was directly above the other, was a very small tin wheel on an axel, the ends of which were inserted in the quills. Holding it up before all, he said that it was an illustration of a great principle in mechanics, and was an evidence of mechanical genius in the inventor.

"If," said he, "one shall put his mouth to zis long quill and blow, ze little wheel vill go round von way—but suppose he puts his mouth to ze short quill and gives von grand—vat you call him? *suck*, eh?—give von grand suck, it vill turn about ze other way. Try it, mon ami," he continued, handing the concern to a herculean down-easter.

All gathered around to witness the experiment, but it was noticed by some that the contriver of the machine began to back out of the crowd.

Down-east put the long quill to his lips.

"Blow vare hard," said the Frenchman, now outside of the throng.

Down-east blew, and forthwith there came out of the short quill, which was pointing directly at one of his eyes, a great cloud of *soot*.

Never was an eye blacked more quickly by human agency.

With an angry oath the victim threw away the box, and cast his available eye about for the great mechanician. He was nowhere to be seen. How our countryman did curse while he rubbed his eye! He denounced Frenchmen individually and collectively, socially and morally.

The general mirth which the affair excited, did not serve to allay his wrath. Finally he took off his coat, and went in search of monsieur, to black *both* of his eyes, he said, with something else than soot. This his friends would not allow, saying it was only a joke, and he must not disturb the peace because he happened to be the victim of it.

And by-and by when the worst was over, the Frenchman came forward and apologized. He said the soot went into the eye, contrary to his expectation, etc., etc., with numerous bows and gesticulations. So good feeling was once more restored.

Had the Maine man, instead of blowing into the long quill, sucked upon the short one, he would have had his mouth and throat filled with soot.

The little tin wheel revolved neither way. The only thing that went round was the laugh, and that was in obedience to a law of nature, and had nothing to do with mechanics.

Feb. 27, at six o'clock in the morning, land was

seen from aloft. The announcement created a sensation for it was *the land of California.*

I was at that moment engaged in duty that I could not desert, and it was an hour before I could indulge my curiosity. By that time the land was visible from deck. The morning was dull and gloomy, and the distant shore seemed to me to partake of that dullness and gloom.

The passengers were giving it their whole attention. They regarded it solemnly, earnestly, and, no doubt, with great satisfaction.

We sailed on all the long day, and just as the twilight was deepening into darkness, we entered the famous Golden Gate.

Two or three vessels were in company. Pretty soon a little craft ranged up on our larboard quarter, and a voice in the gloom asked—

"Do you want a pilot?"

"Certainly not," was the reply.

Something was muttered about a "branch," and then the voice subsided, and the little vessel disappeared in the darkness.

At ten o'clock we anchored, having made the passage from Bath in 173 days.

Thank God! Our weary voyage was at an end. We had reached Eldorado at last. And, save two, we were *all* there.

The veil of night was drawn over the bay, the

fleet, the city—over everything. We saw lights twinkling where the darker shade denoted land, but that did not abate curiosity—it only stimulated it. So, very wisely, we turned into our berths and and waited for the morning.

CHAPTER XV.

BAY OF SAN FRANCISCO—CURRENTS OF THE PACIFIC —"MISSIS BROWN"—SAIL FOR HONOLULU.

As soon as I awoke in the morning I turned out, and, without bestowing much time upon my toilet, hastened out upon deck. The sun was just rising. I turned towards it—not to worship, but to have a starting point at which to begin my survey.

I looked and saw — ah, how treacherous is memory! I cannot remember half that I saw, though I gazed, and gazed again, until every surrounding object should have been indellibly daguerreotyped upon my mind.

What I do retain, however, is very vivid yet. Just under the sun, and fairly rosy in his early beams, the land swept from the eastern shore of the bay, back to the base of Mount Diabolo. That mountain, a very striking object, rose high in the air, overlooking everything between the coast and the Sierra Nevada Range. Between it and the bay, gigantic, solitary trees grew here and there.

I turned slowly to the south and all this changed into a forest of masts. And such a forest, sure, was never anywhere seen before. "The pine hewn on Norwegian hills, stood with the pines of Maine." Side by side with the pitchy growth of the Carolinas, was the evergreen growth of far Australia. No *jardin des plantes* could be more variously constituted. Representatives were there from every quarter of the earth—from the primeval groves of Oregon—from lands bordering on the Okhotsk sea—from the St. Lawrence valley—and from the opposite shores of the Mediterranean sea. They were the masts of ships, and barques, and brigs, and schooners, but both spars and hulls were mingled into a vast and confused mass.

A bold promontory shut out the greater part of the city from view. Rough, uncouth dwellings dotted the shore along where I could see it, and similar ones stood back upon the slope.

To the west, as I continued to turn, I beheld the strait, through which we had entered the previous evening. On the south side an old dilapidated fort, watched, but did not guard, the way, and on the north the shore was high and steep. Next my gaze wandered into the bight of Sausalito, and then over the long stretch of water running up to the tributary bay of San Pablo. Many small vessels were under way in that direction and gave a home-like aspect to the scene.

When I had completed the whole circuit from east round to east again, I drew a long breath like one who has learned the catastrophe of a story.

The entrance to San Francisco bay, prophetically called the *Golden Gate*, by the Spaniards long ago, is wonderful.

In approaching it you sail along the forbidding coast, which appears continuous far as the eye can reach, and seek in vain for an indication of an opening.

But suddenly, as if by magic, it is all before you, cleft by Omnipotent power through the array of rocky hills. At its narrowest part, the passage is only a mile wide. In length it is about three miles: *i. e.*, from the sea to where the bay begins to unfold itself. A very strong tide runs into it. Ships outward bound, when a westerly wind is blowing in, often heave to in mid-channel and let the ebb tide run them out.

The bay within is over sixty miles in length and will average ten in width. It receives from the N. E., through the Bay of San Pablo, the waters of two important rivers, the Sacramento and San Joaquin. On the S. E., also, a little stream flows into it, the river Guadalupe. A few islands lie in it. Whoever has visited San Francisco will remember Islands de los Angeles, Los Alcatrazes, and Yerba Buena. The bay lies parallel with the coast outside, and its entrance, the Golden Gate, is situated not far from midway between its northern and southern ends.

I dwelt at some length upon the currents of the Atlantic and their influence upon the climates of adjacent countries. There are corresponding currents in the Pacific that produce corresponding results there.

The Pacific equatorial current is very broad, extending twenty-six degrees south of the equator and twenty-four north. It flows through the scattered groups of islands that lie in mid-ocean, and, striking the shore of Australia and New Guinea, turns towards the north.

The "Black Stream," the Gulf Stream of the Pacific, pouring through the Straits of Malacca, runs along the coast of Asia, past the Philippines, and the Islands of Japan, striking the American coast just south of the Aleutian Islands. From thence its course is south again towards the equator.

West of California, and just north of the Sandwich Islands is another Sargasso sea, bearing upon its bosom the sea-weed and drift-wood of the north Pacific.

Like the Atlantic currents these Pacific currents distribute the surplus heat and cold of the tropical and polar regions, where they add to the salubrity of the climate, the fertility of the soil, and, consequently, to the comfort and happiness of man. In this distribution California comes in for a generous share.

In what I have heretofore written, I have not represented my duties as being very arduous. I was a sort of supernumerary. But when our anchor fell from the cat head in San Francisco Bay the entire aspect of things was as much changed as if an enchanter's wand had been waved over the ship. The passage was up, and those who had worked their passage rallied no more at the call of "*all hands.*"

On the morning after our arrival the ship's company consisted of the captain, two mates, the cook and the steward and five boys.

Several passengers, while arrangements were progressing for their journey to the mines, preferred to remain on the ship, and work for their board. With their assistance the lumber was discharged quite rapidly. A little was landed at the city, but the greater part was discharged into small vessels and carried away inland.

On board of one of these vessels the doctor found some of his beloved gin. His volubility indicated what the matter was.

The supper hour arrived but no bell rang to

tell us that the tea was made. I was sent to the galley to assist and hurry matters up. On entering I found the doctor sitting on his bench in front of the stove. No sooner did I appear than he began:

"I'se mighty glad you'se come in, Massa R. I'se been tinking 'bout my wife, and 'cluded it's time to send her a letter. Spose you're handy at such tings, Massa R., an' I'll jes' get you to fix up one. Missis Brown 'll be desperate put out not to hear from me, and den, what her relations tink! Dar's Jule Johnsing, one ob de—"

Here I contrived to interrupt him, mildly though, for it flattered me very much to be called *Massa*, and asked to write a letter.

"Doctor," I said, "it's about supper time, and I've come to help you. What shall I do?"

"Well, Massa R., if dey's hungry, we'll get de supper now, and talk 'bout dat letter afterwards. I want you to write it, dough, or I dunno what Missis Brown do, or what her relations tink."

"Shall I lay the table, Doctor?"

"Yes. But Massa R., I hopes you'll tink 'bout dat letter. Missis Brown—"

But I was out of hearing. Supper was soon ready, for there was enough cooked. All the time the Doctor kept up a running fire of words. His ideas were in a very chaotic state, however. I could distinguish as I hurried to and fro

"Baltimore—de ole colonel—Missis Brown—de Johnsings—mos' beautiful head."

After tea was ready I remained in the cabin to wait upon the table. I left the Doctor standing in the galley door, with arms folded and tongue wagging briskly.

When supper was over I picked up an armful of dishes and proceeded forward. The Doctor had disappeared from the galley door, and not a solitary word did I hear spoken within, as I approached. Ah! the second change which marked his courses of drunkenness had come. He was sick. The images of his wife and her relations had all departed, even in that short time. He thought no more about them, nor did he seem to care, then, what they thought about him.

He was reclining upon his bench, and supporting his head upon one hand. He addressed me in a very small, faint, melancholy voice:

"I'se bery sick," said he. "Won't you ax de capen to git me suffin out ob de medicine chest?"

The next day I cooked for the white men and nursed the black man, who was excessively ill. But the day following that, Henry Brown "was himself again," quiet, inoffensive and industrious.

It was not long before our number was reduced

to four, viz., the captain, my brother, myself, and the cook. The mate and steward were discharged, and the others ran off. On an average, however, this was a large number to be left on one ship at that port at that time. In many cases *all* ran.

I landed at one other place besides the city during our stay at San Francisco. One Sabbath day my brother and I rowed the boat over to the little island of Alcatrazes. I have not attempted to describe the city, but I will, Los Alcatrazes, because it can be done briefly. It was composed of uneven rocks, little deposits of guano were on it, screaming birds flew over it, and from it proceeded a horrible stench. We did not stay long.

April 5, 1850, we were ready (with the exception of shipping a crew,) for sea again. The ship had been chartered to proceed to Calcutta, and load for London. It was soon found *impossible* to procure seamen for the voyage to the East Indies. A mate was secured, and that was the extent of what could be done in that direction. The next best thing was then tried, which was to get men to go as far as the Sandwich Islands. Once there we hoped to be able to get some kind of a crew. In this next best thing we succeeded. Six men were shipped on the following terms: The extent of the voyage should be Honolulu, in the Sandwich Islands, the pay one hundred dollars for the run, to be paid in silver coin, on the capstan, as soon as the ship was fairly out of sight of land. It was not at all difficult to understand the present condition of our six men, nor to guess what their future designs were. They had been to the mines and dug out little fortunes. Thus enriched they had returned to San Francisco. The call of dissipation is irresistible to a sailor, and through the avenues of drinking and gambling their fortunes soon stepped out. Then their eyes, and their desires, turned towards the gold region again. But the way there was long, and money was requisite. They had no money. Could they get any? Yes, easily. They could wheel dirt in a wheelbarrow and get five dollars per day for it. Sailors roll no such wheels, however. Then they could work on ship board in the harbor, and receive sixty dollars per month. That was better. But they could also go to the Sandwich Islands and receive one hundred dollars for the run. If an opportunity offered for them to work their way back again, they would have the hundred dollars intact on their arrival. If that opportunity did not offer, the price of a passage was only thirty dollars, which would leave them seventy on their arrival. So it was a sure ticket to the mines either way, and a *sea voyage* had in the bargain. One can easily conceive how an old tar might yearn for that sea voyage—yearn for the luxury of a storm at sea—to hear the music of the gale—to catch a view of the blue, fathomless ocean—and to inhale that air which has no taint of the land.

On leaving San Francisco we numbered eleven, all told. My brother was made second mate. It seemed like the beginning of a long and melancholy task when we manned the windlass brakes to weigh the anchors; but a boat's crew came to our aid from the barque Midas, of Warren, Me. Then the volume of our windlass songs were doubled, the rattling of the iron pauls was quick and continuous, and the last anchor was soon apeak. About ten in the forenoon we gathered away in the ship. When we were able to look out upon the ocean through the narrow entrance, the horizon presented such a threatening appearance that the course of the ship was not altered, and we stood over to Sausalito and anchored again. It was two or three days before our anchor was lifted again. On one of these days my brother and I landed, and took a short walk. The earth was baked hard, and in some places wide and deep cracks appeared in it. But while such was the uninviting character of the earth beneath, there was spread over it by the tasteful hand of nature, a most beautiful carpet of green leaves and bright flowers. None of the plants had attained more than an inch in height, and, as nearly all were of that height, the surface was very even. The predominating color was yellow. The impression made upon my mind by the compact order in which these plants grew, and the coolness and beauty with which they invested the parched and cracked earth, remains to this day.

April 30, we were under sail again, and working out to sea against a westerly breeze. The ebb tide was running out furiously, and thanks to it, we were soon clear of the land, and stretching away to the south-west. According to agreement, six hundred silver dollars were then paid to the crew.

CHAPTER XVI.

ARRIVE AT HONOLULU.—A SAILOR'S ECONOMY.—THE SANDWICH ISLANDS.

AFTER a long, but pleasant passage of twenty days, we saw, one morning, the mountain summits of Oahu before us. The wind was light, and it was not until five o'clock in the afternoon that we anchored off Honolulu. Early in the morning a pilot came off to take the ship inside of the reef, into the inner harbor. The passage in between the reefs is very narrow, and the prevailing winds blow almost directly out.

We got under way, and stood off until the ship's head would point to windward of the entrance, on the other tack, and then went about. When we were abreast of the passage, the helm was put down, and the ship, with her sails shaking, shot into the opening. Then the order was given to clue up everything upon the run, and this was accomplished before the ship lost her way.

Meanwhile a heavy line had been run to the reef on the starboard hand, where a host of Kanakas were in waiting. These all seizing upon the line, drew the vessel along, until she was far enough in to fetch by the reef on the port side, then the line was cast off, everything sheeted home, and the anchorage made under sail. It was lively work while it lasted.

When the ship was moored, our six men were free. Before them lay the town, teeming with sinful allurements. They seemed to understand how far they were from being proof against temptation. The object for which they had undertaken the voyage was yet to be accomplished. They *must* save enough of money to get back to San Francisco, and from thence to the mines. How to do this was a question that they discussed earnestly. One old tar spoke out, as I happened to pass them:

"I'll tell ye, mates, what *I'm* going to do. The rest of ye may do as ye please. The boy here (meaning me) will take care of my shiners while I land and take an observation. Then if it's pay money to San Francisco, I'll pay mine the first thing, and be sure of that much." Two others, younger men, approved of this plan. The remaining three had some other crotchet.

Forthwith those who had constituted me guardian of their treasure came with it. Each one had his hundred dollars in a stocking—a woolen purse. They said they had each taken ten dollars to pay current expenses, and that they would return for the remainder as soon as they had made arrangements for returning to San Francisco. I accepted the trust quite proudly. The stockings I placed in my chest and locked them up. In an hour all were gone. The next day the two young men who had left the money with me, returned. They said they had secured passage to San Francisco in a barque about to sail for that port. The price of a passage was thirty dollars, and they were intending to pay immediately.

The succeeding day the old, veteran tar came on board, and with him a strange sailor. Both had been drinking. In descending the gangway steps to the deck, each made a low obeisance by falling headlong down. After a few words of greeting, the old sailor told me in a husky voice that he wanted money. I brought his stocking. It would seem that the strange sailor had solicited a loan.

"Jack," said the capitalist, opening his stocking, how much do ye want?"

"Say that yerself, my hearty—I'm easy."

The holder of the stocking thrust his hand into it, and drew out a heaped handful of dollars.

"Will that do ye?"

"Yes. Count 'em."

"I'll be cursed if I do, now. Figerin's for landsharks! If ye want more, say so."

"There's a plenty, shipmate. Now when'll I pay ye?"

"There, belay that! No such lingo atween us. Pay when you can pay."

In the transfer of the coin from hand to hand several dollars fell to the deck, but neither took any heed of them. After putting a handful in his own pocket, the owner of the stocking handed it back to me, and the twain were moving off.

"Look here," said I; "see these dollars on the deck. You'll pick them up?"

"Pick them up yourself, if you want them." And the drunken, irresponsible men were soon on their way to the shore. I gathered up the scorned dollars, put them back into the stocking, which had lost much of its fullness, and locked the whole up again.

Two days afterwards the old sailor came again. This time he was silent and morose. He said he would take the stocking altogether, and not trouble me any more. I asked what arrangements he had made for getting back to San Francisco. He said none, and as he did not appear at all communicative, I said no more. When he received his stocking he opened it, and taking out three dollars, offered them to me. I refused them, and said he had given me no trouble. Without a word he threw them upon the deck, turned, and went over the side.

I never afterwards saw one of the six, or heard of one.

We now set about overhauling the ship. Three native riggers were engaged; and a few days subsequently, a young American was shipped to remain by the vessel until she should reach the United States. His name was Joseph Bacon. Though only seventeen years of age, going to sea was the third occupation in which he had been engaged. He had first been a circus rider, then a shoemaker, and he was now a sailor. He had come to the Sandwich Islands in a New Bedford whaleship, from which he ran at Hilo, in the Island of Hawaii. From Hilo he had come to Honolulu, and the American Consul sent him on board of us.

Shortly after Joe came on board, we had a more valuable addition to our ship's company. John C. Oliver, a native of Bath, Maine, joined the ship as carpenter. He was very intelligent, and possessed a great deal of practical knowledge. His experience had been most varied. He had served as carpenter in merchant ships, and men-of-war, had been a speculator in eastern lands, a gold digger in California, and a resident of the Sandwich Islands. The work of refitting progressed quite rapidly. The situation was favorable, the days long and pleasant, and the air invigorating.

The Sandwich Islands were discovered by Capt.

Cook, towards the end of January, 1778, and named thus in honor of Lord Sandwich, at that time Lord of the Admiralty. They are ten in number, and are called respectively, Hawaii, or Owhyhee, Mowee, Tahoorowa, Ranoi, Morotoi, Oahu, or Woahoo, Atooi, Tehoura, Onecheow, and Orechoua. There are various ways of spelling these names. I have written them as they were spelled upon the chart of that region. Hawaii is by far the largest of the group. Tahoora and Orechoua are very small islands, and lie near the opposite ends of Onecheow. The area of all the islands is between six and seven thousand square miles.

The Sandwich Islands are of volcanic origin. Geographers make this remark of all the Islands of Polynesia. "Those which are mountainous are of volcanic origin; the low ones are the work of the coral insect."

Mount Kilauea, an active volcano on Hawaii, is the peer of Ætna, Vesuvius, or Hecla. Extinct craters are numerous on all the islands.

Volcanic countries have one general appearance wherever they exist. The Sandwich Islands abound in rugged, irregular, picturesque mountains, smooth plains, and rich valleys teeming with luxuriant vegetation. The natural products of these islands are the cocoa nut, yam, taro root, sweet potatoe, etc.

It is said that, when first discovered, there were

neither insects nor reptiles upon them, nor any animal larger than a hog. However, the domestic animals of civilized nations were soon transported thither, and they are appreciated by the Islanders. I am in doubt which the Kanaka (who owns both,) loves most dearly, his canoe, or his horse.

The climate of these Islands is delightful. The skies are cloudless, and the atmosphere clear and bracing. Thunder storms are rare, and light. The temperature there, it has been observed, is that which is most conducive to health. There are evident reasons for all this. These islands lie along the northern limit of the Torrid Zone, in the midst of a glorious sea, and swept over by the constant trade wind. Their climate cannot be the same as the climate of a part of a continent situated in the same latitude. The surrounding ocean constantly modifies the temperature.

When Capt. Cook first visited Hawaii, he found the natives rapacious and inhuman. His valuable life was destroyed by them in the most barbarous manner. They were cannibals, and they also offered human sacrifices to their gods. These victims were prisoners taken in battle, however. Others were neither eaten, nor sacrificed. Idolatry was abolished in 1819.

The early Christian missionaries on these and other Islands of Polynesia, in performing their

Divinely appointed labor, have had obstacles to contend with of which we have no adequate conception. When obstacles are mentioned in this connection, our thoughts are naturally turned to the natives, and we expect to discover the most formidable hindrances there. But this view of the matter is not correct. The mass of these people, like those to whom Peter preached on the Day of Pentecost, *"gladly received"* the words of the missionaries.

Let us look in the opposite direction. Could an intelligent and ingenuous heathen be set down in this country to-day, and his conversion attempted, might we not expect him, beholding the laxity of morals and the frequency of criminal acts, to say: "Wherein is *your* religion better than mine, if these are the fruits of it that I see around me?"

So in these distant islands, the ingenuous natives pointed the missionaries to the agents of *commerce*, many of whom were neither chaste, nor honest, nor temperate, and asked, "Are these the fruits of your religion?"

They did not realize that of a people *one* in other respects, a part served God, and a part did not. On this account, among these untaught beings, the licentiousness and crimes of men having the color, and speech, and customs of the missionaries, was something that told terribly against the missionary cause. That was one obstacle. There is another that sprung from the same seed.

The missionaries *must* stand between the vicious of their own people and their victims. This conduct rendered them objects of hatred to those they thwarted, who abused them there, and tarnished the records of their labor when they reached home.

Such evil reports were brought home and published by some of the old navigators. Prominent among these was Capt. Kotzebue, of the Russian Navy. It will not do, however, to bring against him the charges of licentiousness and crime, but investigation *has shown* that, in looking at missionary labor, his vision was warped by excessive prejudice.

CHAPTER XVII.

AT HONOLULU.—A KANAKA CREW.

THOUGH Hawaii is the largest island of the group, Oahu has secured the Capitol. Honolulu is situated on the south-east side of this island. It is narrow of necessity, the sea in its front, and the mountains in its rear not being remote. The harbor is large enough to contain about a hundred vessels, and is formed, as I have said before, by coral reefs. These reefs are submerged at high tide, and bare at low water. The harbor is perfectly secure. The chief street of Honolulu leads out into the Nuuanu Valley. Through this picturesque opening in the mountains, a road extends about six miles, and terminates suddenly in the Pali, a sheer descent of about eleven hundred feet. From the deck of the ship we could trace the general direction of the valley. A little to the right, rising close in the rear of the town, was a high hill with a long, level summit. Along this a tier of guns was placed, and at its south-eastern extremity the Hawaiian flag was daily set upon a tall pole. Farther to the right was the Devil's Punch Bowl, the crater of an extinct volcano.

The town presented, on week days, a very business like aspect. The most noticeable buildings were a stone church, and a new market house, built of coral, from the reefs forming the harbor. The fort could not claim attention as a fortification, but it was interesting on account of its historical associations.

It had played its part in the bullyings which this realm has received from, and the cessions it has made to stronger powers, from the time of the first cession of Hawaii to Vancouver, down to the last French raid. These barbarities seem to have been individual acts, rather than national, and no enduring wrong was done to the infant State.

I went over to the fort one day with the intention of "going round about, and telling the towers thereof," but a squad of Hawaiian troops manœuvring near by took my thoughts completely away from it. These Kanaka warriors were uniformed in a very chance sort of a way. Some sported hats, shirts, and pants, while others had only the hat, or only the shirt, or only the pants, or *neither the hat, shirt, nor pants*. Some handled muskets, others flourished sticks. Their proficiency in drill was about on a par with their equipments.

Whether these were *regulars,* or *militia,* I could

not determine, for it was the only military display I witnessed there.

Our ship was moored fore and aft in the harbor, forward by the anchors, and aft by the kedge to the reef. Right astern of us, not far from where our kedge lay, was a Kanaka hut. It was almost afloat at high water. Its inhabitants were men, women, and children, and quite a number of them; and why they had taken up their abode with the fishes, as it were, I could not imagine. Perhaps they were not fit to live with other people. Certainly they were not an amiable family. They had repeated quarrels, and the air was filled with their hard words; often they filled it with something harder than words, stoning each other for hours, sometimes.

I witnessed one of these quarrels one day from aloft, where I was at work. A poor wretch of a girl was up to her middle in the water on the reef, and the others were stoning and reproaching her from the hut. Had she desired, she could have taken herself out of the way very quickly, for these creatures swim like fishes.

Frequently the stern hawser would shake, and on looking over, I would behold a naked brown body, climbing upon it, out of the water.

It is a favorite pastime with the Kanakas, generally, to go down to the shore where, and when the waves were rolling in most furiously, and dive under them, coming up two or three hundred yards off, outside of the surf. When they return they commit themselves to the highest wave, and ride to the shore on its crest. They often carry with them a piece of board which they bear before them in their hands. From the deck of the ship we could see their dark bodies plunging all day long into the white surf that broke on the reefs. It would not be much out of the way to say that a Kanaka is as much at home in the water as on the land.

Their canoes are formed from trunks of trees, and invariably carry outriggers to stiffen them. The canoe is their national craft, and they are, of course, skillful in the use of it.

Nothing occurred to bring us into contact with any of the higher class of natives, excepting that two young men, connected with the Royal family, and students of the Royal School, came on board one afternoon and remained until evening, taking tea with us. They were very fine appearing men, quite polished in their manners, spoke good English, and were social and companionable. It was said that many of the chiefs were amiable gentlemen.

Of the mass of the population not much complimentary matter can be written.

We remained at Honolulu until the twelfth of June—about twenty days. My duties were too pressing for me to see much outside of the town, save what was visible from the ship. One Sabbath, however, I thought it but just that I should have a run. So I mustered my available cash, put on my best suit, and stepped into the boat, which was about to proceed to the shore for something. From the landing I directed my course towards the fortified hill I have mentioned, in rear of the town. After passing out from among the buildings, I found myself upon a beaten path, leading to the foot of the hill. The surface of the ground was already slightly ascending. While walking briskly along, I was suddenly taken "all aback" by a scene at the roadside. Three native women were lying asleep in the gutter. The mud was soft enough to take impressions, and they were making fine ones.

It may strike some that these women were as naked as the swine they were imitating. Not so, however, or my astonishment would have been less. They were dressed—not in mats of their own manufacture—not in the skins of beasts, birds, or fishes —*but in the richest and most gorgeous colored satin.* Strange anomaly! Whence are they, who are they? I wondered, and straightway I had thoughts of King Kamehameha's household. But looking still more closely, I abandoned that idea, for the dresses, though so rich in material, were entirely without proper form, mere bags with lesser bags for sleeves.

Inquiries made subsequently, enlightened me in regard to the matter, but I cannot venture upon an explanation.

Turning away from these human swine, in their congenial mud, I pursued my way toward the hill. Before me no one was coming whom I might meet, and no one going whom I might overtake; nor was any one following me, near, or in the distance. A Sabbath calm had settled down upon the country, the town, and the shipping.

The road led up the southern slope of the hill. Though quite steep, the ascent was not difficult for one whose wind was good. The view from the summit was magnificent, and I stood admiring it long after I was rested. At my feet lay the town. Beyond, decked with flags, rose the masts of the shipping in the harbor. Outside, the waves of the great ocean broke in white foam on the reefs. On the left, was the Devil's Punch Bowl, and groves of cocoa nut; and back of me, on the right hand, the dark peaks of many mountains. Over all a cloudless sky hung, and down upon all the great sun poured his vivifying and cheering rays.

In making my survey of the summit of the hill, I first walked from end to end of the long row of cannons. Each muzzle was flush with, or projected over the brow of the hill. They were twenty-four and thirty-two pounders, and all in poor condition.

Had the guns been in good order, it would have been a very effective battery. It overlooked the harbor and the roadstead, and in a measure, commanded all the approaches to the town.

I was surprised to find no person on the hill. The stronghold seemed to be abandoned. Where the flag staff stood was higher than the level of the guns. About it was a great pile of cannon balls. As I moved in that direction, I heard a slight, unusual sound. It was neither the rustle of the flag, nor the sighing of the wind. A few more steps revealed the cause. On the ground, by the farther edge of the pile of balls, an old Kanaka lay on his back, asleep. A little solo that he was performing on his nasal organ had reached my ears. I walked about the old fellow, whistled, coughed, and rattled the cannon balls, but he slumbered on without the quivering of a muscle. Now, thought I, suppose I were a cruel, designing, relentless enemy to the Hawaiian kingdom, and the Hawaiian king. I could capture and dismantle this stronghold in about thirty minutes, and inflict any indignity upon the standard of the realm. I would first take up a cannon ball, and dash it upon the head of the sleeping Kanaka, a process calculated to scatter his brains pretty promiscuously about. (I will insert here, parenthetically, that the above calculation about the Kanaka's brains was altogether erroneous. I was not aware at that time of the thickness and solidity of a Kanaka's skull. Subsequently, as I shall have occasion to relate in the course of this narrative, my eyes were opened. If a thirty-two pound ball *had been* dashed down upon this sleeper's head, it would probably have roused him from his nap, but it would not have hurt him much.)

Let me see—the last thing I did before entering the parenthesis, was to knock out the Kanaka's brains, in imagination. That done, I would descend to the level of the guns, and shove them, one after another, over the brow of the hill. Then I would take down the Hawaiian flag, and tear it into pocket-handkerchiefs—after which I would amuse myself by rolling the cannon balls down after the cannons. If Kanakadom came to the rescue meanwhile, and I could not frighten them by rolling balls at them, I would flee over the other side of the hill and seek a place of safety.

However, being a friend to the Hawaiian kingdom, and in no wise an enemy to the Hawaiian king, I attempted no such thing.

When I left the hill the Kanaka was sleeping the sleep that knows a waking, the flag of Hawaii blew out proudly from its staff, and the cannons still overlooked the town. And yet my imagination was so fired by taking the fortress, that I found myself absolutely compelled to do something unusual and heroic. Therefore, instead of descending by the road, as I came up, I went over the brow of the hill, straight towards the town. It was very steep —in places almost perpendicular. It was "a hard road to travel." I regretted that I had on my best suit. Otherwise I should have sat down, and cautiously "put her through to the bottom." But my apparel had to be spared. So I stamped along, driving my heels in as far as I could, feeling and testing everything before I committed my weight to it. Once in a while I would find a stout tuft of grass in just the right place to lead me over a perpendicular jog. When nearly down, I caught sight of a man walking swiftly toward me from the town. I began to think my proceedings were irregular, and his object was to call me to an account. I kept on, however, and met him a little way from the foot of the hill. He was a young Kanaka. When he passed me, instead of frowns, his face displayed smiles. I was very tired when I reached the landing place. Two Kanakas offered to paddle me on board, and I graciously permitted them to do so.

When we were about ready for sea, a crew was shipped consisting, according to articles of agreement, of a boatswain, *and ten able seamen.* But the facts of the case were these. The boatswain was but an ordinary seaman, and of the ten men, not one had ever put foot upon a ship's deck before.

Some one may wonder how we came to be so deceived in them. We were not deceived, except in the boatswain, whom we supposed to be a thorough seaman.

I have already said that men were not procurable in San Francisco, to go far from that attractive place; and suitable men were not to be obtained at Honolulu. If any were there, their faces were set towards the East, Eldorado, and not towards the West. We knew, beforehand, all this to be true of white men, but we did hope to find at the capitol of the Hawaiian kingdom, Kanakas who had been taught seamanship and English by the whalemen, who often employ them on board their ships. We were disappointed, because many ships had preceded us, bound to the same ports, and having the same necessities as ourselves. These had gleaned from *all* the Islands every man who could handle a marlin spike, or climb a mast. We were, therefore, compelled to take what we could get, and on rather hard terms, at that.

In the boatswain we considered we had a treasure. He was a native, he said, and a thorough sailor, and understood and spoke English. Here, then, was one to interpret to the others, and teach them what it was necessary they should know.

The ten green Kanakas were furnished to order by the King. It was said he furnished them in any quantities to the crewless ships. We had ours upon the following terms. They were to receive twenty dollars per month, and one month's pay in advance. Here again rumor (which is the same thing, and as often correct in one place as another,) dragged in the King. It was said that he received the whole, or the greater part of this advance, and it was the price for which he sold a subject.

He did not sell them unconditionally, though, as will be seen by another item in the terms. Each Kanaka, unless he left voluntarily, or died, must be eventually returned to the Islands, or five hundred dollars forfeited for him. Bonds were required to that effect. It would have been a hard case, had the men actually been seamen. How much more so, then, when it is understood that they literally **knew** nothing. And then such names as they had!

CHAPTER XVIII.

MORE ABOUT OUR CREW.—SAIL FROM HONOLULU.—VARIOUS MATTERS.—PROPOSED ROUTE TO THE INDIAN OCEAN.

I WILL in a few sentences complete my description of our Kanakas. I referred to their names. Two only were able to retain their patronymics throughout, viz., Cuhaver and Lolo. Chance, or some peculiarity of the individual, soon fastened new appellations upon the others, and they bore them thereafter, while with us.

At one time I had seen and been fascinated by a picture of John Gilpin, that "citizen of credit and renown." He was represented as he appeared when "the trot became a gallop soon in spite of check or rein." I retained, and still do, a very vivid recollection of the picture, and no sooner did my eyes rest upon one individual of the ten, than I involuntarily exclaimed, "*John Gilpin!*"

There was no resemblance in point of flesh and rotundity—right the reverse; but it was the position of the body, and the peculiar cast of all the limbs.

The name obtained, and he was henceforth known as "John Gilpin." This worthy's age had been given as twenty-eight years. One gazing on his indescribable face, and observing how squarely it was framed of great bones whereon was no flesh, would have said "a centenarian," for there was nothing juvenile in his appearance. That face of his was near akin to Death's head. It was almost frightful.

"There's an old customer," said the carpenter, referring to John Gilpin.

"Only twenty-eight," I said.

"Hoot!" said he, "I have seen him before. He is reputed to be vastly more than a century old. Look at his teeth. (They were not quite as large as gravestones, as were the Giant "Eat-'em-all's," nevertheless, they were uncommon teeth.) They say," continued the carpenter, "that he helped to eat up Capt. Cook—the old rascal!"

By the way, what did become of Capt. Cook's flesh? His *bones* were recovered. For what purpose did the natives remove the flesh? Might it not have served them for a meal? Remember they were cannibals, upon the captain's own authority.

Another Kanaka was called "Big Man." Why? *Because he was a big man.* Another was dubbed "Dan Gideon." Why, again? I don't know, I'm sure. "John Steward" was the name bestowed upon the youngest; and the most intelligent of the ten was known as "Little Bill."

June 12th the pilot, an old Englishman of the exact complexion of a carrot, and of the exact shape, from the shoulders down, of a short, thick one, came on board. We unmoored and made sail. Instead of passing out canal fashion, as we entered, we glided swiftly out between the reefs before a brisk breeze. Just outside we hove to. The pilot's boat was hauled up to the gangway, and wishing us a quick and pleasant passage, he descended the side —the oars of his Kanakas fell with man-of-war's precision, and the boat shot back into the harbor.

"A quick and pleasant passage!" Oh, pilot, pilot, pilot, could we have foreseen how different must be our fate from your kind wishes, sad indeed would our hearts have been!

We filled away again. The wind was fair. Sail after sail was spread as quickly as our awkward crew could work. All the long day we labored, expostulated, and *gesticulated*, but the sun was far down before the anchors were secured, chains stowed, and order restored about decks.

There had been laid in, for ship use, quite a stock of squashes, potatoes, and pigs. Particularly did we have a large quantity of squashes. The rail across the forward part of the poop deck was closely hung with them, and the quarter boat nearly filled.

Joe Bacon and myself, representing the more youthful portion of our little community, had privately catered for ourselves, and our purchases, in the shape of cocoa nuts and watermelons, were stowed away in a berth in the forward cabin.

Cocoa nuts are about one thing the world over; but there was something about the flavor of the watermelons of Honolulu, "all their own." I had eaten them at home, and, I regret to say it, had stolen them from the neighbors' gardens and eaten them. And at the Academy and at college, I have since aided in the consumption of these vegetables (how obtained does not matter now), but never have I met with any, anywhere, at all comparable with these of Hawaiian growth. Had they too, been stolen, and possessed the added sweetness of stolen fruit, they would have rivaled Ambrosia.

After supper, filled with a spirit of observation, I went forward to see how the Kanakas came on. It was their supper time, and I found them congregated between the foremast and the windlass. Two or three were eating from a large panfull of stewed beans, but the greater part were sitting about in a delightful state of sea-sickness.

All at once the ship gave three or four unaccountable rolls. The first was not violent, and nothing moved on deck, but the second was violent, and pitched the sea-sick Kanakas down against the rail on the port side. The third roll sent the well Kanakas down upon their already prostrate companions. And the barrel which supported their bean stew, losing its bearings, pitched the bean dish bottomside upwards upon the poor fellows—hot gravy upon cold meat. The ship, rolling with increasing violence back to starboard, nearly threw me from the forecastle. I caught by the paul bits, and, luckily, held on. Every moveable thing on deck was in motion. With a grand crash and rattle, a number of empty barrels dashed about between decks. The iron hooks of the blocks, as the opposite yard arms pointed, now up, and now down, grated in the eyebolts, and the blocks themselves thumped heavily on the yards. The iron trusses of the lower yards snapped and squeaked, the chain topsail sheets clanked against the yards and masts, the square sails spilled, and the jibs threshed against the stays. All this occurring at that mysterious hour when darkness has half gained the mastery over light, brought ten thousand undefined terrors to the souls of the Kanakas, and to the universal uproar they added their demi-savage groans, shrieks and expostulations. Just then the Doctor issued from the galley to see what was to pay. He had been eating his own supper, and the interruption provoked him; but he was rendered doubly indignant when he beheld the fate of the supper he had prepared for the Kanakas. His accustomed silence was broken.

"How's dis?" he said to the Kanakas, who were trying to regain their feet. "Been a eatin' wid de hogs? Spose you eat wid 'em all de time? Dey's de neatest ob de two, dat's sartin. I'll ask de cap-en to hab a big trough made. If dat's de way de beans go, dar won't be many 'board dis ship afore soon. Jes' go right 'long an' clean up dat ar mess, now!"

Having relieved his mind, the Doctor returned to finish his supper. It was a ridiculous scene, taken altogether, and pretty soon the well Kanakas began to appreciate it. First, sundry diabolical grins were interchanged, then followed pantomimic action, and then barbarous words, and, at length, by way of pleasantry, they made feints to, and actually did lick the bean soup off from each other.

It has been a mystery to me ever since, what caused the ship to roll so furiously, just then. Save the long ocean roll with which we were running, the water was not much agitated, for the wind was light. She had rolled none before during the day, nor did she any more after she was through with those violent vibrations. It might have been that the helmsman let her swerve so far from her course that the long swell came on her quarter.

Through the night the weather was pleasant and the wind light. And the succeeding day was also very pleasant. After breakfast the arduous task of drilling our crew commenced. They were mustered upon the poop deck, and the boatswain instructed to harangue them to this effect:

"You will now be taught how to make and take in sail, and you must pay particular attention, and learn to do it all very well and very quickly."

The mizzen topgallant sail was then clewed up. The attention of the Kanakas was called to the halliards—how the yard was raised and lowered by them; to the clew lines—how they gathered up the corners of the sail; to the buntlines—how they raised the foot. Then they were told that what was done with this sail was a common process with the other similar sails. They were then exercised in furling it.

Next the mizzen topsail was taken in hand, reefed, double reefed, and furled. Then both sails were set again. This was repeated several times, both in the forenoon and afternoon. As we were running directly before the wind, this practice upon the sails of the mizzen mast did not affect the speed of the ship. Lessons were also given the Kanakas in steering.

The next day the exercise was resumed, and they were additionally drilled in hauling up the courses, handling the jibs, etc. These exercises were continued many succeeding days, Providence favoring us with fine winds and weather, for what we had to do.

One or two of our scholars, Little Bill, in particular, showed some aptitude, catching quite readily at names and ways of doing things. But by far the greater part had a natural fund of stupidity, which neither art nor perseverance could exhaust. Especially was this true of John Gilpin. If he was told to find even the main topsail halliards, he would turn in every direction, with a ghastly grin on his anatomy of a face, thrusting his hands in this way, and that. As for finding the halliards in question, he could not do it. Practice, far from making him perfect, did not enlighten him in the least.

A very mortifying fact came to light during this course of instruction in nautical art. We soon noticed that the boatswain, although he spoke in a tongue unknown to us, did not seem to be well understood by the Kanakas, whose countryman he had represented himself to be. At length their misunderstandings became so great that the matter was investigated. After much ingenious inquiry it was ascertained that Mr. Boatswain was *not* a Sandwich Islander, but a native of Tahiti. The Kanakas could comprehend a part of what he said, but not all. Whether they understood from a similarity of the Hawaiian dialect to the Tahitian, or the boatswain had partially mastered the former, I do not now remember. One way or the other it must have been, for while they understood him in part, they were also perplexed in part.

Knowing the bloodthirsty character, and piratical tendencies of the natives of the islands among which we were to pass, my father had purchased in Honolulu, several army muskets, and an abundant supply of powder and ball. The carpenter was also directed to construct a carriage for a brass four-pounder which was on board.

When the carriage was completed and the gun mounted upon it, it was remembered that, to be effective, something was required in the loading besides powder. We had plenty of that, but no cannon balls. "Necessity is the mother of invention." There were on board several tons of *spikes*, varying in length from four to ten inches. We made up parcels of these, and they proved on trial, to be very formidable missiles.

It now occurs to me that I have not designated by what passage my father intended to pass the East Indian Archipelago. He had never navigated those seas, and had, therefore, asked advice, and consulted many authorities on the subject. He was generally advised to sail by the Gilolo and Ombay passages. It was declared to him that fair winds, fair currents and fair weather, prevailed there at that season. Just consult the proper map in the Atlas, and you will see the direction in which we were to go. The Gilolo Passage lies between the Island of Gilolo and the small islands lying around the northern end of Papua, or New Guinea. To reach the Ombay Passage from there, one must sail through Pitt's Passage, by the northern end of Bouro, and thence southward across the Banda Sea. Ombay Passage is between Timor and the small Island of Ombay, to the north, and leads into the open Indian Ocean.

The advice received in regard to this route was backed up by books. Miserable, miserable advice it was, and lying books they were that confirmed it.

CHAPTER XIX.

ILLNESS.—A MUTINY.—THE LADRONES.

THE twenty-second day of the month I became ill with dysentery. It might have been brought on by eating too freely of watermelons and cocoa nuts. Who can always say, however, whence disease comes?

I only know that this came with unusual violence. It was after six in the evening when I experienced the first unpleasant sensation. At four, the succeeding morning, so much had it prostrated me that, while crossing the cabin, I fainted and fell. My father, who was present, raised me and laid me upon the transom in his state room. Just above me (a cause for gratitude in that hot clime,) was a window that admitted cool air. As days passed by, to increasing helplessness was joined mental aberration. When taken ill I was reading, for the first time, Cooper's "Last of the Mohicans." I had reached the point where Hawkeye and his inseparable friends rescue Duncan Heyward's party from the grasp of Magua, on the summit of the mound whither he had led them. Of course I had been absorbed in the tale. What boy, reading it, for the first time, is not? And now my wandering mind went forth to mingle in the stirring scenes described and to engage with the same actors in new ones. I participated in the eventful night in the cavern on the rocky island at Glenn's. My blood was curdled by the strange sounds, which, rising from the river's bed, Hawkeye declared not to be of earth. When day broke, I fought the Hurons across the tumbling water. I conversed with Chingachgook, with Hawkeye, and with Uncas, as though they were always by my side. And so, for days, I lived in an unreal world. Beings who had no existence were my companions—my haunts were strange localities, thousands of leagues away. Yet through all this I saw, darkly and dreamily, the real world about me. I knew that disease was wasting me away. I saw, dimly, my father and brother moving before me. I could discern pity upon their countenances, and often anguish. I was conscious of the bounding motion of the ship, and the rain pattering upon deck, above, made grateful music in my ears. After a few days, my mind returned from its wanderings. The first violence of the attack had ceased, and languor and listlessness succeeded; but the disease was unchecked. The usual remedies prescribed for such cases were powerless, and I soon became feverish.

Then water was denied me, in accordance with the old time custom of treating fevers.

We were in the Torrid Zone and under a vertical sun. Of course it was hot—hot as the breath of a furnace. Oh, how hard it was to lie there and wrestle with my fierce thirst! By day, all my thoughts were of water. I called to mind the many pleasant springs upon the old homestead. I saw them gushing out from the cleft ledges. How well the mental eye replaces what the physical eye has lost! I seemed to stand by one particular spring in the field, whose cool, clear water I had often drank. I watched it bubbling up from its reservoir which was never exhausted. The gray sand rose and fell, moved by the gushing water. The green grass swayed and waved about the margin. The golden buttercups nodded; and, just within the bounds of hearing, the wind passed with a rustling sound through the leaves and branches of an ash. Now balancing on his wings, and now alighting on a twig of elder, a bob o link was caroling his joyous song. The great sun was overhead, and not a cloud floated in the clear, azure heaven. What dispelled this pretty illusion? I knelt down to drink. As I bent nearer and nearer my face was mirrored below me; but when my lips were almost touching, fancy took flight, and the hard reality, burning thirst and no water, only was left me. Then, with all my remaining strength, I would toss myself on my hard bed, and moan.

By night, when I was sleeping, it was much the same. I dreamed of water. Then I was, of course, more comfortable than during the day. That fierce sun was then set whose beams heated, to an unbearable degree, the atmosphere about. But water is required to slake thirst, and no sooner did I sleep than I thought of it in dreams. Often I seemed to be in Rio, walking by its pleasant fountains. Great thirst had made me extravagant. I drank water by the hogshead. But the waking dispersed all such luxurious fancies. Oh! there is no humanity in an idea that denies water to any living creature. May they be few who perish of thirst!

Once in a while I was permitted to moisten my throat with water in which burned bread had been soaked. That was something, but it was far from quenching thirst.

In my pain, weakness, and bewilderment, I lost all knowledge of time. The light told me that day had come, and the darkness that it had gone again. And a day seemed intolerably long—more like a week, or month, than just a day.

The carpenter, who possessed no mean skill in medicine, was consulting physician. Where there is no regular physician on board a ship, the captain is physician, *ex officio*.

I grew rapidly worse. "The undiscovered country from whose bourne no traveler returns—that universal asylum where the wicked cease from troubling, and the weary are at rest," was, seemingly, not far off from me.

But at length they brought me a remedy, of which my recollections are indistinct. The proper quantities were given me at the proper times, and very soon the disease was checked. When it became evident that I was really recovering, the carpenter informed me that the last remedy was a desperate one, and that, while he had *one hope* that I would rally, he had *nine fears* that I would die. I don't remember what my sensations were when this revelation was made, but, undoubtedly, I saw reason for rejoicing.

One day as I lay half asleep—and consequently half awake—there came from the fore part of the ship a thundering report. The cabin windows rattled, and the ship herself quivered.

"What was that?" I asked of the first one that came near.

"The cannon. This is Independence Day. We have the colors up, too."

"Where are we?"

"Just to the eastward of the Ladrone Islands."

With this information I was again left to my reflections.

Not long thereafter, a bustle on deck drew my attention. I listened, and presently knew that the studding sails were running down. Soon a current of air, cool and refreshing, poured through the open window above my head. Then a hoarse sound was audible without. A rain storm was rushing along the water. Soon drops fell on the deck overhead, at first slowly, then fast and furiously. Lulled by the sound, I fell asleep. When I awoke the rain had ceased. My father was standing near by.

"We have had mutiny on board," he said.

"When?"

"To-day."

And he told me the circumstances:

Just after meridian, the weather appeared squally. It was advisable to begin to reduce sail early with such a crew, and the order was immediately given to haul down the studding sails. This was done under the supervision of the mate. While engaged in making up the foretopmast studding sail, he became so enraged at the stupidity of the Kanakas, that he kicked one fiercely several times. Instantly the sail was dropped, and the whole posse laid violent hands on him. The boatswain, also, sprang from the other side of the deck to aid in the launch overboard—for overboard they designed to put the mate. But, as he sprang forward, a rope rolled under his feet, and he fell so heavily on his breast

across the breech of the gun, which was in front
of him, that the blood gushed from his mouth and
nostrils. By this time the Kanakas had gathered
the mate up in their arms, and had him near enough
to the low rail of the forecastle to say " Launch
Ho," had they been sailors, and known English
enough. Not a word was spoken, however. The
Kanakas were silent from policy, the mate from
pride and mortification. In this desperate emergency,
the carpenter came bounding to the rescue.
Coming up from his bench between decks, for something,
he had seen the perilous condition of the
mate. Springing to the forecastle with the speed
of thought, he knocked down three of the savages.
The mate was dropped, and, luckily, inboard. The
Kanakas turned upon their new enemy. And to
their aid young John Steward came rushing from
the galley, with great enthusiasm. He mounted the
forecastle, caught up a capstan bar, and directed a
blow at the carpenter. This was easily eluded, and
before John could recover from the force of his own
blow, the pale, slim carpenter planted his fist between
his eyes, and he performed a complete back
somersault off the forecastle, and fell head foremost
into the wash-deck tub on the main deck beneath.
At this point, the condition of affairs was observed
from the poop deck. Joe Bacon was on the end
of the spanker gaff for the purpose of painting it.

My brother had just hoisted a keg of paint up to him, by the ensign halliards, and my father was hauling taut on the spanker vangs, to steady the gaff. The two latter immediately ran forward, and Joe, dropping his brush into the bucket, grasped one of the vangs, slid down, and followed after with all speed. But before they could reach the scene of action, the conflict was renewed. This time the combatants were on the main deck. The mate, grasping a stout axe handle, which had been used for a heaver, strove to regain his lost reputation. But he was soon thrown down, and ignominiously jerked about the deck by his hair, legs and arms. The reinforcements coming up, the battle became general.

On one side was legitimate authority, represented by five whites and one black man—for the Doctor had issued from the galley grasping his long iron poker. On the other side was rank mutiny, personified by nine tawny savages. The issue was not long doubtful, however. The presence of the captain seemed to stagger the mutineers. They had a wholesome fear of his office, and his gigantic proportions were also greatly in his favor. In a few minutes the foremost Kanakas were forcibly and securely ironed, and the remainder surrendered at discretion.

A review of the field gave the following list of

casualties: The boatswain was severely hurt by his fall. With admirable tact, he changed sides, and declared he fell while hurrying to rescue the mate. The contrary was known, however. Four Kanakas had swollen eyes, and a fifth, John Steward, had a large piece of scalp knocked off by coming in contact with the wash-deck tub.

On our side (I say *our*, because my sympathies would have been enlisted had I known what was transpiring,) no injury was sustained, save that the mate's hair was shockingly pulled.

The next step, of course, was to sit in judgment on the offenders. But a glance to the westward forbade all deliberation. In that quarter both sky and water had assumed a threatening aspect. Dark clouds hurried up, and spread themselves along the heavens. The north wind fell down. A hard squall was at hand, and the ship under full sail. One course was necessary with the refractory Kanakas. Briefly and earnestly the captain informed them through the boatswain—an imperfect medium, but one that answered—that any more violence would be punished by instant death—that guns and pistols, and powder and ball, were plentiful in the cabin, and that henceforth there would be no delay in using them. So they must look out.

The irons were then taken off, and all hands ordered to take in sail. Away went the Kanakas, headlong, treading on each others' heels, all zeal, and all cheerfulness.

The whole thing proceeded from dislike to the mate. If any heart on board really contained anything regularly mutinous and sinister, that heart was in the breast that was bruised on the gun—the boatswain's. Thenceforward, however, he controlled himself. His hurt was internal, and did not heal. While with us he was weak, and bled often at the lungs, and when he left us, at Calcutta, it was evident that his life must be short.

As for the Kanakas, it was, probably, their intention to finish making up the studding sails after they had thrown the mate overboard. Beyond an impulse to take vengeance for the kicks and blows they had received, they were innocent, I think, though they did seem to act in concert.

The affray demonstrated that a Kanaka is not formidable in a rough and tumble fight with a white man. His aim in such encounters is to grapple his opponent, hug him, and break his limbs. He does not seem to have any conception of a trip or a blow. And when he sees a bit of his own blood he is disheartened. I may not present Kanaka pugnacity correctly, but exactly as it displayed itself in our crew.

July 5th Guam was in sight away to the north. This island is one of the largest of the **Ladrones**, and lies farthest to the south. Magellan so named these islands on account of the thievish disposition of their inhabitants. Ladron is a Spanish word, and signifies a thief or a robber.

They are also called the Marianne Islands, from a Queen of Spain who sent out missionaries to convert the heathen.

This group seems to have been much frequented by the old navigators. Besides Magellan, their discoverer, Clipperton, Anson, Byron, Wallis, and others visited them. They were discovered in 1521, and pertain to Spain.

CHAPTER XX.

"SWINGING ROUND THE CIRCLE."—A QUESTION OF
TIME.—GILLOLO.—A HARD HEAD.

JULY 20th, we passed within sixteen miles of Mariere, an island lying near the north-east entrance to the Gillolo Passage. The days intervening between the *fourth* and twentieth had given us a sad experience. We found we had been wholly deceived in regard to the navigation here, at this season of the year, at least. The prevailing wind was a westerly one, and we encountered not less than a three-knot current setting to the north-east, a deflection of the great equatorial current, caused by the dense congregation of islands. In the sixteen days we had gained only about 800 miles. It was discouraging—the more so, because contrary to expectation. The sixteen days, however, had wrought better things for me than for the ship.

When Mariere came into view I was able to go on deck and behold it. There can be no doubt but every rational being, who does not actually desire to die, is, after illness, very grateful for the return of health. At least, that was my experience.

Let me now give, briefly, an account of our progress for the eleven days immediately succeeding. Our course lay W. S. W. for the Gillolo Passage, which I located in a former chapter. Let it be remembered, now, that such was our course and our position (sixteen miles south of Mariere) at noon of July 20th. And also, let it be borne in mind that all that men could do to press the ship forward upon her course, was done.

Well, at noon of the 21st, we were 55 miles to the south of Mariere. At noon of the 22d we were 45 miles S. S. W. At noon of the 23d we were 100 miles W. At noon of the 24th we were 176 miles N. W. by W. At noon of the 25th we were 175 miles N. W. At noon of the 26th we were 185 miles N. W. At noon of the 27th we were 240 miles N. W. by N. At noon of the 28th we were 200 miles N. N. W. At noon of the 29th we were 60 miles N. E. by E. At noon of the 30th we were 50 miles E. N. E. *At noon of the 31st we were 12 miles S. by W.* The circuit was completed. We had circumnavigated Mariere. The 20th had gone, the 31st had come, and in the interval, a period of gales and calms, we had gained nothing. We were four miles from our position of the 20th, but no further on our way. Mariere, to which we had said farewell on the 20th, was nearer on the 31st. In 27 days we had gained 800 miles—about 30 miles a day. Was it not discouraging?

It was afternoon when I went on deck a second time to look at Mariere. Though nearer than it was before, nothing could be distinguished about it, save a very well defined outline. It is a low island, round in form, and about two miles in diameter.

It was far from being a pleasant day. The sky was dull and overcast. The ship was running towards the N. W. under easy sail. Now and then the branch of a tree, or its trunk, or its roots, or the whole tree, would appear floating. Such must have come from the islands away to windward. All these objects were surrounded by multitudes of little fishes, and occasionally we saw great, bulky turtles lying alongside of the trunks.

I was much better in health than when Mariere lay in view before. I was stronger, and appetite returning. Blood was thickening, and flesh and fat growing again.

As the ship glided by branch after branch, I remembered that such things once testified to Columbus of an undiscovered land. It was easy for me, under such circumstances, to fancy that I saw the eager Admiral, impatiently pacing the deck of his vessel, glancing now down at these tokens of land in the water, then forward, as if he would overcome space by the sense of sight, and discern the place of their nativity.

Well, good bye again, Mariere. Thy name should have been *Miserere*. Then how appropriate would it be upon our tongues!

Towards night the wind changed more to the south, and held in that quarter until the following night. With this wind we could run for the Molucca Passage, north of Gillolo, at an easy bowline, while we could not head up for the Gillolo Passage by several points. Under the circumstances it was decided to abandon the latter route for the Molucca Passage. Both led into Pitt's Passage.

At the end of forty-eight hours we were 250 miles from Mariere. This was such good progress, comparatively, that a glow of encouragement came over all. In the exuberance of our joy it was resolved to scale the gun. To test its efficiency in shattering piratical proas, a charge of eight-inch spikes was put in. On the weather bow, about 400 yards off, was a bunch of sea-weed. This was chosen for a mark. The carpenter was also gunner. He trained the piece upon the floating mass, and at a signal from him, it was discharged by the Doctor, who used for a linstock his poker, one end of which was red hot. For an instant the air was rent by the whistling spikes, then fragments of the sea-weed flew up as the dark water grew white beneath the plunging missiles. We possessed a more formidable weapon than we had supposed. Such a discharge would have destroyed any ordinary boat.

It is said that firing at sea will raise a breeze. The light air blowing when we shot at the sea-weed immediately hauled dead ahead, and increased to a gale. The ship, under short sail and away down on her side, made as much leeway as headway. Our encouragement changed to discouragement. Once more we "swung round the circle." August 9th we were only 135 miles from Mariere. Mariere—*Mariere*—always MARIERE. I won't write that name again!

A furious current ran to the north-east, as rapidly as four miles an hour, certainly. You will admit that it was discouraging.

After the 9th the wind came from the south again, and we began to move in the right direction once more. On the 12th, we found that we were at fault somewhere in calculating the position of the ship.

The fact was, that we had gained the better part of a day by sailing so far to the westward. So we made no account of the twelfth day, in the Nautical Almanac, but strode across it to the thirteenth. That regulated our reckoning. Does any one ask how that could be? Suppose that here, in Ann Arbor, I held a portable dial in my hand, and when the shade upon its face marked nine o'clock Saturday morning, should, with the exact *apparent* velocity of the sun, pass to the westward around the earth. Every moment of time the shade would indicate nine o'clock upon the dial. And, consequently when I had made the circuit of the earth, and reached Ann Arbor again, it would still be nine o'clock Saturday morning, *with me*. But with you it would be far otherwise. On your dials the shade would creep up to twelve, then retire to six, or seven, and the sun would disappear. Those "lesser lights that rule the night" would succeed. At midnight, a new division of time would be ushered in. In their turn, the stars would disappear, and the sun would rise upon Sunday morning. Again the shade would begin its slow march along the dial face. When it indicated nine o'clock, you would exclaim, "Nine o'clock *Sunday* morning." "No," I should say, "it is Saturday morning. I have seen no sun set, or rise." But I should be wrong, you see. It would certainly be *Sunday*. I had consumed a day, but its consumption was not indicated to me by any of those changes which mark the passage of time.

So to us, steering ever westward, contrary to the rotary motion of the earth, more than twelve hours of time had passed imperceptibly; but, though we had not regarded it before, it now became necessary to do so.

Edgar A. Poe's story of the "Three Sabbaths in One Week," illustrates this loss or gain of a day by the circumnavigation of the globe.

On this day, which was ostensibly the 12th, but really the 13th, we passed Cape North, on the northern end of Morty, ran round the northern extremity of Gillolo, and entered the Molucca Passage. Each of the above mentioned islands were visible as we passed. To afford us an agreeable surprise, the wind hauled to the S. E. The ship lay her course S. S. W., down the passage. The Talenading Islands came into view and disappeared on our larboard hand. The water was smooth and the wind light. We were surprised to find whales numerous here. In every direction their spouts were to be seen dissolving into mist.

The 17th we passed the Islands of Tyfore and Meyo, leaving them on the starboard, or right hand side of the ship. They lie about twenty-four miles apart, and a little more than a third of the way from Gillolo over to the north-east end of Celebes.

Aug. 20th we crossed the Equinoctial Line for the third time. Nine days from that time we were in sight of the Island of Little Po Oby. Between the Xulla Islands and Oby Major, the passage is narrowed down to about thirty miles in width. We had worked down the west shore of Gillolo, about 200 miles, against gale and current, and through calms, and thereafter that island would lie astern of us.

And here I shall presume so much upon the ignorance of some of my readers in East Indian geography, as to give a little description of the Island of Gillolo, which I have mentioned so often.

It is one of the largest of the Moluccas, or Spice Islands, containing about 6,500 square miles. It cannot fail to strike the eye, upon the map, on account of its grotesque form. Taking the middle part of it alone it is not uncommon, but when we tack upon that, on the south, a very long, slender peninsula, and upon the north, a shorter and more corpulent one, and upon the north-east another one still, it becomes remarkable. It is not altogether unlike some large, awkward bird upon the wing— a goose, or heron, for instance. The north-east peninsula would represent the tail, the northern peninsula and the middle part the wings, and the long southern peninsula the neck. This disposition of the parts, however, leaves nothing for a body. It cannot, then, altogether resemble a goose; but it may a heron, for the *hull* of that bird is exceedingly small compared with the length of its *spars*. This singular form is thought to be the result of violent volcanic action.

Gillolo, like many of the adjacent islands, rises abruptly from an unfathomable sea. This is, in a measure, fatal to the productiveness of the land bordering on the sea; for the rich soil created by the decomposition of the volcanic rock, is washed into the ocean.

Gillolo is situated in the torrid zone, a small part of it to the south of the Equator. Its climate, therefore, is subject to but little change, but is always hot and unhealthy upon the lowlands, always endurable upon the upland slopes, and always delightful upon the hills.

The precious spices, cinnamon, cloves, nutmegs, and pepper, are among its vegetable productions. It produces, also, the breadfruit tree, cocoa nut palm, bananas, and yams. It also has the more common products of that clime, such as rice, sugar, cotton, etc. Its chief exports are sago, edible birds' nests, honey, beeswax, sandal wood, ambergris, turtle shells, mother-of-pearl, pearls, and gold dust.

Its animal productions are not uncommon. Reptiles and insects are numerous. Those questionable pets, the monkey and the parrot, are natives. The birds are remarkable for the brilliancy of their plumage. The Bird of Paradise is found here, and on many of the adjacent islands.

The human inhabitants are quite numerous, and are of two races. In the recesses of the mountains live the native race. Little is known of them, save that they are a kindred race to that which inhabits

New Guinea. Their conquerors, the Malays, possess the sea coast. They are a treacherous and bloodthirsty people.

Gillolo belongs, nominally, to the Dutch.

What I have said of this island is true also with regard to the other Moluccas, save as to its size, form, and locality.

We continued to work slowly along. Sept. 3d the Island of Xulla Bessy was in sight on our starboard bow. Just after midday, we had a shower from the south, after which the wind died entirely away. The air, cooled by the rain, was clear, refreshing, and delightful.

I was looking to the south, whither our course lay, and whither, as a natural consequence, our hopes and desires pointed—and, happening to raise my eyes somewhat, I saw a dark object standing in bold relief against the sky in that direction. Could it be the Bouro Dome, or Tomahoe Mountain, so distinctly marked on the chart? Others looked and saw the same. It was quite seventy-five miles distant. How I longed for a nearer view! And I felt that my longing would assuredly be realized. A little time, and a breeze of wind would accomplish it.

This day I had evidence of the solidity of a Kanaka's skull. I was standing with my father at the break of the poop deck. The Doctor's voice spoke from the pantry beneath—

"You John, dar." (John Gilpin, being useless lumber as a sailor, had been turned over to the cook's department, as assistant.)

In response to the Doctor's call, the skeleton head of John Gilpin appeared at the galley door. The eyes looked aft, and the mouth grinned.

"Fotch de baker pan," said the Doctor. Then in an explanatory way—"To put de bread in, you know—de biskits—hangs on de larboard side—*dat* side (gesture, probably), ob de stove." The head was drawn back into the galley. A moment passed, and the Kanaka came in sight forward of the house, carrying the wash-deck tub.

"Dat a pan?" said the Doctor. "Tote dat back —get de pan—get de baker pan—put de bread in. You gwine to be a fool all de time?"

Away went John Gilpin a second time, and returned with a bucket.

The Doctor's voice again—"What you bring now? Dat's a bucket. I gib you jes' one more chance. Fotch de pan—de baker pan.

This time John brought a pot.

"Go 'long," said the Doctor. "I fotch de pan myself."

"Oh, you—you—" my father burst out. "What are you good for?"

Then snapping the rope yarn that held a squash

to the rail, he raised the squash and hurled it at John, shouting—

"Take that, you brown scoundrel, and get out of my sight."

The squash flew through the air, and, striking John on the side of his head, was shattered into many pieces. The shock never jarred John, but he was frightened, and rushed precipitately into the galley.

The transaction forcibly reminded me of the sleeping Kanaka, whose head I fancied I could crush with a cannon ball. Doubts now arose in my mind as to whether I should have succeeded in that undertaking, or not.

CHAPTER XXI.

BOURO DOME.—REEFING TOPSAILS.—THE MILKY SEA.
—CUHAVER RAMPANT.—IN SIGHT OF COPANG.

YES, it was Bouro Dome, whose summit we had seen so far above the horizon. Sept. 4th, we stood out by the southern end of Xulla Bessy, to the westward, and on the 5th, having caught a favorable breeze, reached a point within twenty-five miles of this object of my admiration.

The next morning we lay becalmed right under the shadow of this magnificent mountain. On the western side, the sea washes its base. It was well called Bouro Dome, for apparently, no more symetrical dome ever was conceived in the mind of man, or constructed by man's hand. While we lay in the calm sunshine—happy to be becalmed just there, since becalmed we must be—some one aloft shouted—

"Sail ho!'

"Where away?" was eagerly asked, for it was a rare cry with us in that locality.

"On the starboard quarter."

That was toward the south. Looking sharply, we saw it from deck, a mere dot or speck, on the glassy sea. It was decided to give our neighbor a gun, to let him know he had Christian company in these remote seas.

The gun, which had been taken down from the forecastle, was accordingly charged, and the muzzle thrust out of a port on the starboard side. Bang! There was a ringing in our ears, a trembling of the ship under our feet, while the wave of sound swept outward over the calm sea.

A faint, hollow roar returned from the foot of the mountain, but the still sea had no echoes to be disturbed, and the report, after reaching the ears on board the distant ship, died away in the distance.

It had been evident for some time that, with never so good a chance, we could not reach Calcutta without a fresh supply of water. About us were no convenient ports. My father had a bias for Amboina, a Dutch settlement, a little more than three degrees to the eastward. And if our southerly wind was to continue, no place was more convenient than that.

Again the firing was quickly followed by a breeze. As usual, it came from the south, directly ahead. Soon, however, it changed to the eastward and increased in force. It seemed to leap in fierce gusts from the mountain down upon the sea. The light sails were immediately furled, and then came the order to reef topsails.

The fore and mizzen were settled away—the yards rounded in to spill the sails—the reef tackles hauled out, and amid the clatter of ropes and threshing of canvass, we sprang into the rigging. I was now well and strong enough to be of some service. My aim, when I got in the rigging, was for the weather earing of the mizzen topsail. I knew it was a pretty easy place to sit, for I had been there often. But I was not smart enough this time. My brother passed me in spite of my best efforts; and then I was compelled, either to take the lee earing, or shirk a duty that custom imposed upon me. I began to regret my hurry since I could not hurry enough. I always had a horror of a lee earing, and had never hauled one out. However, I went *down* the yard to leeward, caught hold of the lift, threw my right leg over outside of it, and settled down as comfortably as I could on such an uncomfortable seat. The ship was away over on her side, and the yard, as far as a perpendicular position went, to all intents and purposes, a cock-bill.

Making the best I could of the matter, I thrust one long leg through between the leach of the sail and the reef tackle, twisting the other up in the foot rope, and went to work. While they were hauling out to windward, I got my earing clear, took a turn with it, and then found I should have a moment's leisure to look about.

I first put my hand behind me and felt the end of the yard on which I sat, and twisted around and looked at it. It seemed to have grown short and small, all of a sudden, and I thought it anything but a luxurious seat. As I looked at the yard, my eyes rested for a moment on the water over which I sat. It was in wonderful commotion. The old ship would right up a bit, then a fiercer gust would spank her down again, and she in turn would spank the water with her counter, and roll off a ridge of foam. A glance at the deck showed me the captain at the wheel, roaring out to the carpenter, and three or four Kanakas, who were manning the gear of the main topsail. And right in front was Bouro Dome—no, *Tomahoe Mount*, I will call it now—looking grim and inflexible like the genius of the storm. Surely, within its bowels must be situated the "vast cave" where "King Æolus controls the impatient winds and sounding tempest." Their murmurs, under the restraint of their monarch, are audible. Will he continue to restrain them? Or will he smite the enclosing walls and unchain them, and sweep our good ship like a Trojan hulk, a wreck, along the sea?

Think not it required as much time to see these things as to tell of them. It was only a wandering glance, the space of an ordinary breath. Then the reefers yelled "haul out to leeward," and I, having hauled in the slack of my earing and wound it around one hand, took hold close up to the cringle with the other, and, throwing myself backward with all my force, yelled, "*haul out to leeward.*"

I got no more glances while there, for when I had passed the first earing and fastened it, and cleared the second, they were ready to haul out to leeward again. But my sense of feeling and my sense of hearing, both, told me that the main topsail halliards were started. It was a big, heavy piece of canvass, that main topsail, but the wind played with it as if it had been the merest bit of ribbon on a girl's hat. Thresh, thresh, it went, and every spar jumped in concert. But machinery and skill prevailed, and it was soon quieted.

Slowly we surged off from the angry, windy mountain. To double reefs succeeded close reefs. The main sail was furled, and the foresail reefed. By-and-by everything was furled except the main spencer and fore topmast staysail.

In the darkness, the foam that covered the sea showed ghastly white. We ventured to think that such a gale, long continued, would land us on the coast of Celebes. We had Capt. Woodward's narrative of his captivity there, on board, and had read it. We were quite willing to credit all that he said, and did not desire at all to have such scenes come under our own personal observation.

Contrary to our expectations, but in conformity with our wishes, the wind abated after midnight, and worked back to the south. We made sail, piece by piece, and at noon tacked in shore again. At five P. M. we were well in with the land, with all sail set. We had altered the bearing of Bouro Dome four points. It bore now N. E. But it was a perfect dome, look at it from what direction we might.

It was pleasant sailing that afternoon. The water was smooth, and there was just a good wholesale breeze blowing. Every sail was set that would draw on a wind, and with a good rap full, we went racing in.

Reader, have you sailed much in small sail boats? If you have, you will remember how, when close in to the land, and standing directly for it on the wind, a boat's speed seems to increase. The water is usually smoother. Gust after gust will come, bending the boat gracefully down, and giving her such a bounding impulse that she seems to leap along. Just so our ship raced in towards Bouro. Objects grew more and more distinct. The indentures of the shore, the paths of rivulets, vast fragments of stone, and the luxurious vegetation, were plainly visible; but we looked in vain for a sign of human existence. There was nothing—no habitation, no appearance of cultivation, no proas floating in the little bay. Let no one suppose, however, that Bouro was not inhabited. Just now a careful observer would have detected something unusual in the movements of all hands. In silence the mate gravitated towards the forecastle; in silence the second mate scrutinized the coils of the lee braces; in silence the men gathered in the waist; in silence the Doctor thrust his head out of the galley door. Meanwhile the captain, silent too, paced the weather side of the poop deck. As if worked by machinery, all eyes turned upon him when he walked forward, and turned upon the shore when he walked aft. Each turn the captain's pause at the break of the poop was longer. At length he broke the silence.

"Ready about!" he said, and waved his hand to the helmsman.

Instantly "ready about" resounded fore and aft, succeeded by the falling of coils of rigging upon the deck, and the metallic clank of the sister-hooks in the iron thimbles, as the clues of the mainsail rose. The captain walked aft, and stood by the wheel. Steadily the helmsman turned it.

"Hard-a-lee!" shouted the captain.

"Hard-a-lee!" echoed the mate from the forecastle, and the next instant the flop of canvass in that direction indicated that he had eased off the jib sheets.

The ship's bows came swiftly up to the wind. The current of air drew fairly fore and aft.

"Mainsail haul!"

"Mainsail haul!" repeated many voices, and the yards of the main mast and the mizzen mast were swung with an accompaniment of sound from iron trusses, blocks, ropes, and human throats. The ship, in the smooth water, worked like a fore and-after, forereaching rapidly as the wind against the head sails bore her bows off.

"Let go and haul!" said the captain, rubbing his hands.

The head yards were swung, the wheel was righted, the main tack was boarded, jets of spray began to be thrown from the bow, the ship with Bouro astern, like the canoe of Hiawatha

> "Westward * * * *
> Sailed into the fiery sunset,
> Sailed into the purple vapors,
> Sailed into the dusk of evening.

As soon as we were far enough south to fetch by the southern shore of Bouro, our course was shaped for Amboina. This was the 9th of September. The wind was light, and our progress correspondingly slow. At two o'clock we discovered a sail on the weather beam. It neared us, and we soon made it out to be a proa, running down before the wind. If fears of a piratical craft entered our minds they did not remain long, for the proa kept on her course, and at dark had crossed our wake, and was scarcely discernible on the lee quarter. It was probably a merchant proa, coasting from island to island.

The next day the wind came fresh from the east, directly ahead for Amboina, but a good wind for our proper course. After a little deliberation Amboina was given up, and Copang, on the Island of Timor, a place lying in our way, chosen for a stopping place. So the ship was kept off S. S. W. for the Ombay Passage. The wind gradually freshened, and we made good progress across the Banda Sea. Many whales were visible.

When night came a surprise awaited us. The water appeared to be white—as white as milk. We puzzled our brains for an explanation of the phenomenon, guessing with that recklessness characteristic of Yankees everywhere. But as there was no one to say when we guessed *right*, it was all unsatisfactory.

I quote, as an explanation of the appearance, two or three paragraphs that went the rounds of the papers several years ago. It will be seen that our locality and that of Capt. Trebuchet were nearly the same.

"The French Minister of Marine has sent to the Academy of Science, in Paris, a report of Capt. Trebuchet, of the corvette Capricieuse, in which it is stated that on the night of the 20th of August, 1860, when about twenty miles from Amboina, he and his crew beheld the curious spectacle of the Milky Sea, and what the Dutch call the Winter Sea, because the sky and water present the appearance of fields covered with snow.

"The phenomenon lasted from 7 P. M. until daylight. It was at first attributed to the reflection of the moon, which was then about three days old; but as the appearance continued after the moon had set, this explanation was discarded. A bucketful of sea water having been drawn up and examined, it was found to contain about 200 groups of animalculæ, of about the thickness of a hair each, but of varying length. They adhered to each other like strings of beads, and emitted a light similar to that of the glow-worm and fire-fly.

"It was admitted that the white appearance of the sea was caused by these minute creatures, the number of which must have exceeded all human calculation."

A long time I sat and watched, in wonder, the changed color of the water. When I, at length, turned in, I hoped that the consciousness that we were making good progress would insure a fine night's rest. We were destined, however, to experience a little interruption of that night's slumbers. I was awoke by the noise of a scuffle on the deck overhead. The captain sprang from his swinging cot, and rushed up the steps shoeless and hatless.

I will account now for the noise. It was the mate's watch, and Cuhaver had the wheel. The former lectured the latter severely upon his steering, and not satisfied with that, struck him on the head with an iron belaying pin. Thereupon Cuhaver (unharmed by the blow—another proof of the thickness of a Kanaka's skull,) let go his hold upon the wheel, and threw his arms about the mate so as to pinion that officer's arms completely. Then he began to chant a dismal song, griping more and more tightly his struggling victim. What he intended to do with him, heaven only knows.

At this juncture my father reached the deck. Seeing that the ship would be caught aback unless the helm was immediately put up, he bestowed one blow upon Cuhaver, and ran to the wheel. Stunned by the blow, which took effect upon the left side of his under jaw, Cuhaver fell, with his armful, across the top of a sky-light. Others soon reached the scene of action, and just in time to prevent the mate, who had escaped from the relaxed grasp of Cuhaver, from taking signal vengeance on that dusky savage. Through the remainder of the night Cuhaver wore those peculiar bracelets manufactured for the wrists of refractory men.

In the morning an investigation of the affair was made. In the midst of the testimony, however, the captain broke out in expressions of disgust, and would hear no more. The irons were removed from Cuhaver, and he, with a twisted jaw and swollen face, went about his business. This day the carpenter was added to the mate's watch.

We spent one more night upon the Banda Sea, ploughing its milky waves, and on the following morning made the Island of Ombay right ahead. We then tacked, and stood to the N. E. until we saw the Island of Wetter, laying on the east side of the passage, when we went about again to the south. That afternoon we passed the high, rocky island of Po Cambing, and on the following morning the north-west shore of Timor was in sight. During the day and the succeeding night we ran along the shore, not very far from it.

At ten o'clock the next day the Bay of Copang opened before us. For a little while it was calm; then a breeze began to set shoreward. With the breeze, a topsail schooner came in sight to the south, steering into the bay. As our courses converged, we soon drew near to each other. The spy-glasses were in great requisition, and almost constantly directed in search of the town. Presuming the schooner to be better acquainted with the navigation than ourselves, we furled the royals, hauled up the courses, and fell into her wake. By-and-by, looking carefully, we could discern a little settlement nestled among the trees. It was flanked in one direction by a fortification, and there was a ship lying at anchor in front, seeming close in.

CHAPTER XXII.

AT COPANG.

THE nationality and character of the strange ship were immediately subjects of animated discussion. My father thought it to be some Dutch man-of-war that belonged on the station. The mate and the carpenter inclined to the opinion that it was the periodical Dutch ship, come for the products of the island.

In the midst of the discussion my brother, who was looking through a glass, declared the ship had colors flying. This announcement closed the argument, and the glasses were again leveled at the stranger. All saw the flag, but none could say of what nation it was. The distance was too great. I eagerly snatched the first glass that was laid down, and went with it to the forward part of the poop. Descending the steps half way to the main deck, I adjusted it nicely, leaned it steadily on the combings of the aperture, and applied my eye. I saw bunting waving at the stranger's gaff, but it blew directly from us, and I could make out nothing. I watched narrowly. By-and-by a furtive gust blew it sidewise, and spread it without a fold across my line of vision. There was no mistaking it. I shot up the steps and rushed aft, exclaiming—

"She's an American ship!"

I had seen the stars and stripes as plainly as I could wish to.

"An American ship?" said my father, rather questioningly, looking again through the glass. "Oh, a whaler. I see her boats now."

Soon he caught a view of her flag, and added, "She *is* an American, that's a fact."

We all felt a peculiar satisfaction when it was settled, beyond a doubt, that we had fallen in with our own countrymen.

We passed a small, low, sand island on the right, when within a mile of the shore, came to the wind, and lay with our main topsail to the mast. We lay some time wondering at the apathy of our countrymen, since we had the signal for a pilot flying. At length a boat was discovered pulling off from the shore. It came with great swiftness. When near at hand, we saw that it was a whale boat, manned by white men, and we rightly conjectured that it was the property of the whaleship, and manned by whalemen. The side ladder was lowered. The boat swept alongside, and the officer who sat in the stern came rapidly up the ladder. He announced himself as the captain of the New Bedford whaleship *Phœnix*, and received a very warm welcome.

"You must excuse our tardiness," he said. "I was on shore, and my mate sent a boat for me, supposing that I would prefer to come off to you myself."

Under his direction we filled away, and ran in and anchored to the south of his ship, and about half a mile from the shore.

Copang—written also Coopang, Coupang, Cœpang, and Kœpang—is also known as Fort Concordia. The event most likely to make it a place of interest to the general reader, is that it was the end of Lieut. Bligh's remarkable boat voyage.

He was forced from his ship in the vicinity of the Friendly Islands. From thence to Copang, a distance of about 3,600 miles, he sailed in an open boat, only twenty-three feet in length, six feet nine inches in width, and two feet nine inches deep. The occupants of the boat were eighteen in number. Their whole stock of provisions was 150 pounds of bread, sixteen pieces of pork, six quarts of rum, and twenty-eight gallons of water. After reaching New Holland they landed frequently and obtained fresh food. The time consumed was forty-seven days. The Dutch residents of Copang gave them a most hospitable reception, providing for all their wants.

The day of our arrival was Sunday at Copang,

but Saturday with us; for, though we had made the requisite change in the day of the month, we had not yet changed the day of the week. We did now, however, and the day which began with us as Saturday ended as Sunday.

The ensuing day we commenced operations. My father proceeded to the shore with the captain of the whaleship, whose name I have forgotten. The presence of the Phœnix in this port was of great advantage to us. Her captain, having already been through the process of procuring supplies, greatly aided my father by his advice. Bright and early, the mate turned all hands to on the water casks. We had a busy day, breaking out, striking out, towing ashore, etc.

Copang had her harbor merchants, bumboatmen, or whatsoever they may be called, as well as more frequented ports. Half a dozen soon found their way on board our ship, each intent upon turning an honest penny—*the penny anyhow*—they did not care so much whether it was an honest one, if so they got it. They dealt in monkeys, parrots, and fruits. But we could not negotiate with them that day. "No time," we told them. "No money for trade to-day. Come again to-morrow." They went away reluctantly.

Tuesday, my brother and myself, in company with the carpenter, visited the whaleship. On mounting to her deck, we were greatly astonished at beholding, mixed up with the pigs on the main deck, on the timber heads, on the hatches, in the boats, monkeys—everywhere, monkeys!

The carpenter soon paired off with his brother "chips," and my brother also found his "affinity." I stuck by an old weather-beaten tar, who was very pleasant and gossippy.

"How came you," I asked him, at length, "to buy such a drove of monkeys?"

He laughed. "I'll tell you," he said, "and you'll be able then to get a plenty of them without paying for them. Have they been on board your ship with them yet?"

"Yes."

"Had strings to them and made them fast when they got them on deck, didn't they, and then went hunting and peering about?"

"Yes."

"Well, when they come aboard again, and tie their monkeys, do you, as soon as they travel out of sight, cast the animals loose. That's the way we got our monkeys. They can't catch them again, any more than I can catch this one."

So saying, the old sailor walked slowly up to a young monkey that was sitting on the fife-rail of the foremast, and looking gravely at him. Without stirring or winking, the hairy creature let the man's hand approach him within an inch; then, with a sudden jump, and a loud chatter, he flew up the rope nearest to him. His chatter was echoed from all parts of the ship, and a stampede of monkeys began. They rushed up the rigging—they gallopped along the rail—they raced about the boats—and one, about the size of a child of eight years of age, sprang on the back of a pig, and rode forward, escorted by a troop of his smaller brethren.

I was fairly frightened. My mind was made up at once not to cast any monkeys loose on board of the Hampton, nor suffer any one else to do it, if I could help it. I felt relieved when we returned to our own ship.

This day, having received a supply of coin current at Copang, we made some purchases. The mate bought a young monkey and a paroquet.

Somebody followed the example of the whalemen, and cast loose half a dozen monkeys while their owner was in the galley driving a bargain with the Doctor. They mounted the rigging, with their strings dangling behind. After numerous and persevering efforts, four were recaptured, and the remaining two took passage with us to Calcutta. One more, a small and very amiable monkey—a present to my father—completed our list of these animals.

One article offered for sale here was sugar, done up in a very peculiar manner. A vessel was fabricated of palm leaf on the model of a baker's pan —not quite as long and wide, but of the same depth. Into this vessel the sugar, which was said to be made from the sap of the palm, seemed to have been poured in a liquid state. As it grew hard it naturally adhered to the bottom and sides. At one end of the vessel was a bail, also of palm leaf, by which it was carried very conveniently. The sugar inside had no disposition to drop out, so you see these articles were portable in the highest degree. A man could hang as many of them on his arm as he could carry.

The sugar was of the same color as our maple sugar, and had much the same taste. It was very cheap, one of these vessels filled with it, costing but a trifle.

Wednesday, the driving part of the work being over, my brother and myself visited the town, taking Joe Bacon along with us. Copang consisted of two streets parallel with the beach, and less than half a mile in length. Across these at right angles ran two or three rather devious paths. Through the place, from rear to front, ran a shallow stream of water.

We went first with my father, to the house of a lady with whom his business had made him acquainted. She was Chinese, but spoke English very well. Her husband, who was the principal merchant of the place, was then absent on business in another part of the island. We remained half an hour, hearing the little lady chat. When we rose to depart she gave us a very kind invitation to return and drink coffee with her when it should be noon. This we declined as politely as we knew how, and having said good-bye to our hostess, and listened to some warning words from the captain, sallied forth.

We first turned to the right, and crossing the stream on a rustic kind of bridge, went towards the fort. The entrance was open, and a sentinel pacing in front. We asked if we could go inside. He shook his head. We took this for a negative answer, though I have since thought he did not understand us, and wished to express as much by shaking his head.

Denied admittance, as we thought, we walked around the walls outside. We were not much impressed by the strength of Fort Concordia. It was doubtless intended as a protection against any hostility on the part of the natives. For that purpose it answered very well, but a civilized enemy, with cannon, would soon knock it down. In our circuit we came upon a target which had been considerably riddled by bullets. This target was so placed that the balls after passing through it, or *by* it, according as the shooting was good or bad, struck an angle of the fort. The wall at this point was much defaced.

From the fort we went back across the bridge, and then turning, followed the stream, leaving the town behind. Soon we seemed to be "walking in enchanted bowers." In places, so dense was the vegetable growth that the sun's rays penetrated only here and there. The tree was overhead; the shrub was on the right hand and on the left, and the vine was not only above and around, but also under foot. Where the sun's rays did penetrate, their golden gleams contrasted strikingly and pleasantly with the deep green of the huge fan-like leaves. Out from this cooling shade we stepped, and stood in romantic glades where the sunlight was unobstructed. A few steps carried us across these, and we walked through groves of the tall cocoa nut palm. All around, delicious fruits were growing, and everywhere a pleasant odor was diffused about. Birds flitted from tree to tree, startling the eye by momentary exhibitions of their bright plumage.

We returned to the town, and all our agreeable sensations fled. The men who were born lords of this soil and its gorgeous productions, were not inviting characters. We passed from end to end of the chief streets. On each side, on the thresholds of the houses, sat rows of half naked, swarthy, ferocious wretches. Each held across his lap a long gun, with rusty barrel, and unvarnished and unstained stock, and to the side of each was attached a crooked, ugly-looking knife. They were all motionless as statues, and regarded us with a fixed stare as we passed along.

Why they were squatted down there, from end to end of the streets, we could not conjecture. I think they could not have been inhabitants of the town, but were from the country, and came on business or for pleasure.

The houses near the beach were chiefly stores, and kept by Chinese. At these we made some purchases, and were then ready to go on board. On the beach we encountered some of the whalemen. We told them where we had been, and asked if we had seen all the objects of interest.

"All," they said, "except the Joss-House."

"What is that?"

"Where they keep their idol and have their fire."

The place was at a distance, and a boat was on its way from the ship for us, so we were compelled to forego a sight of the Joss-House, and his honor, the Joss.

Timor is 250 miles long, with an average width of thirty miles, and contains upwards of 6,000 square miles. It is remarkable on one account. A chain of high mountains traverses it, and on the side of this chain towards Australia, the animals bear a resemblance to those of Australia, while those on the opposite side are closely allied to the fauna of Sumatra and Java.

Timor belongs jointly to the Dutch and Portugese. Copang is the chief port. It is easy of access, furnishes good water and plentiful supplies of poultry and vegetables.

The Malays are not credited by authorities with many—indeed, I may say, *any*—virtues. Their chief characteristics are jealousy, pride, cunning, and duplicity. They have a predilection for the sea, and when once on it, if they have the power, and the opportunity occurs, they are, of course, guilty of piracy.

A few months before our arrival, some proas had captured a brig about thirty miles up the coast. All hands were barbarously murdered, and the vessel plundered and burned.

The practice of "running amuck" is a peculiarity of this people. To "run amuck" is to rush ferociously along a street, stabbing, biting, and anathematizing every person who is met. The fate of the person who runs amuck is that which a mad dog meets with us.

I thought there was a fine chance for an exhibition of this characteristic pastime in the streets of Copang. I should have been a pleased spectator as long as I could have been a safe one; but while there was any possibility that a "creese" would find its way between my own ribs, I should have objected to it, and if my objections had been unavailing, I should have removed myself as speedily and as remotely as possible.

As we looked back after getting on board the ship, the place appeared marvelously fair, with its encircling palms, and background of wood crowned heights. But this is a world of compensation. Who would rather be a Malay, among the profusion of the tropics, than an Anglo-Saxon in a temperate zone?

CHAPTER XXIII.

A DESERTER.—DEPART FROM COPANG.—WRESTLING.— ANOTHER HARD HEAD.

WE reached the ship at four o'clock in the afternoon. Before dark a rumor was in circulation that two of the whaleship's crew intended to desert that night, and conceal themselves on board of us. It was our design to sail in the morning. Well, morning came, and scarcely was the sun risen before a boat, well manned, pulled towards us from the Phœnix. The captain was in the stern. He came immediately on board, and after exchanging the usual salutations with my father, unfolded the object of his early visit.

"One of my men," he said, "has deserted. He left the ship last night, and I am almost certain that he came on board of you, and has concealed himself."

"There was a report yesterday," my father said, "that two of your men intended to desert to us. If one *has* deserted, he may be on board, though I have no knowledge of the fact. If you desire to do so, you can search the ship."

"Tumble up here," said the captain to his men in the boat. "We will search for him."

A systematic search of the ship was instituted. No part was exempt, except the cabin. I stood on the poop deck and observed that part of the search which was going on above deck. Two whalemen mounted the house, and peered about under the boats which were stowed there. Not finding anybody, they lifted the folds of the main topmast staysail, which was stowed between the boats. I noticed, as they did so, that a meaning glance passed between them. They said nothing, however, but descended to the deck, and with a brief, "Nobody there," joined in the search in the hold. There the men were equally unsuccessful.

All now gathered about the gangway, and directed their eyes towards their disappointed captain. I said *all* looked towards their captain. I should have excepted one stout, sandy-complexioned, and sandy-whiskered man. He was not, like the others, content with what had been done. Perhaps he was content with what he had himself done; but *he* had not searched any on deck—a part of the ship that now underwent his careful, personal supervision.

He mounted the house and looked perseveringly under the boats. Being so conspicuously engaged, he became the object upon which all eyes were fixed. The group at the gangway turned from their captain to him. The two captains, and all our silent attentive crew, centered their gaze upon the sandy man. He was a sort of forlorn hope. No one spoke a word.

Fruitless was Sandy-man's seeking under the boats. Hopeful still, he tried the staysail. Up came one fold—nobody; another fold—nobody; a third fold—"Ha! here he is!"

Well done! Sandy-man—well done! But why do you descend so hastily from your elevation?

A lithe, active-looking young man rose slowly up, and disengaged himself from the staysail. Looking around, his eyes caught Sandy's retreating form. He jumped from the vicinity of the sail, and shaking his fist at the man, shouted out:

"So *you* want to be a boat-steerer, do you? Just get up here again, and we'll see which is the best man. Curse a man that'll betray a shipmate! Curse a man that'll curry favor with the captain! Oh, you'll be made a boat-steerer for this!"

All this time the young man walked hurriedly about the little space between the boats.

"I dare you," he continued to the man, "to come up here and stand before me. You're bigger than I am, I know, but I won't mind that."

Sandy muttered out something. He did not accept the challenge. He looked—if I must tell it—Sandy looked dreadfully confused. Now the excited man's remarks about currying favor with the captain, *might* have been unjust. This did not appear in Sandy's countenance, however. He held his head down, and did not choose to meet the indignant eyes of his shipmates—for his shipmates did not admire his deed, that was plain enough.

The deserter's harangue was interrupted by his captain.

"That will do, Jack—that will do. Get into the boat now, and we'll go aboard."

"Get into the boat!" repeated Jack, with a tone and countenance of despair—then jumping up and down, and smiting his fists together, he burst forth:

"Curse your boat, and you too, sir! Curse your old ship! I've slaved in her, and starved in her long enough. Here we've been out sixteen months, and havn't got oil enough yet to grease your way to the infernal regions—"

"Hush! hush!" his captain interrupted; "don't make your case any worse—it's bad enough now. Get into the boat at once, and let's have no more of such folly."

"I *won't* get into the boat unless the captain of this ship tells me to. Till he says go, you can't all of you take me off this house."

The whaleship captain stepped back, and my father said:

"You must go into the boat, my poor fellow, for I have no right in the world to detain you."

"I'll ask you nothing for my services, captain. All I ask is to be delivered from—"

"Say no more," said my father, interrupting him, "for it is useless. Your captain has treated me kindly, and aided me in many ways. Without his full consent I cannot take you. I have not the right, the inclination, or the power to do so."

"Farewell, Hope, then," said the runaway; and he slowly descended from the house. "As for you," turning to Sandy, "if I don't be even with you, may I perish."

Poor fellow! I have always had a wish to know what happened to him afterwards. Some of our crew were aware that he was on board. He went on shore first from his own ship, and came off to our's about midnight, in a canoe. Another did intend to come with him, but his courage failed him. The two men whom I saw overhaul the staysail saw their shipmate, but they were unlike Sandy. That worthy, doubtless, had in view a boat-steerer's berth.

After the whaleship's boat had departed, we got under way and went to sea. The wind was favorable, and we soon left all the land astern, and found ourselves sailing on the skirts of the Indian Ocean.

Our progress grew more respectable, and better spirits than formerly prevailed on board. After reaching the longitude of Java Head, our course began to incline to the north.

Going forward one evening, during the dog watch, I found Joe Bacon and the Kanakas good-naturedly discussing Cuhaver's attack upon the mate while we were crossing the Banda Sea. The conversation was carried on in mongrel English phrases, with now and then a brief translation by the boatswain. Joe represented that the mate could not be much, or he would soon have settled his bearish antagonist. As for himself, though he was no fighter, he would like to see the Kanaka who could hold him, even one instant, in anger.

This provoked some bragging on the part of the Kanakas. Finally Big Man said to Joe:

"You nothing—me can make you go down with one hand."

"Not with both, big as you be," retorted Joe.

"Spose try." And Big Man laughed, and all the Kanakas laughed in concert.

"Come on," responded Joe, nothing daunted.

"No fight," said Big Man, "but me make young brag go down."

So he went cautiously up, and laid his great hands on Joe's shoulders. But no sooner did they rest, even lightly, there, than Big Man's heels flew up, and his broad shoulders struck on the deck like a bale of hides. All the Kanakas uttered ejaculations of astonishment and wonder.

Joe had hardly moved. He was a skillful wrestler, and did his work quickly. The Kanakas, having no conception of a trip, could not comprehend what floored their champion.

Big Man got up and rubbed his shoulders. He looked a little confused, but was still good-natured. He proposed to try it again. He did, and went down as quickly as before, and declined a third trial. Joe then challenged the others, but there was no response.

"See this, then," said Joe, and immediately turned several somersaults, some forward and some backward. These feats, remnants of his circus performances, enhanced the astonishment of the Kanakas. They gave him credit for superior powers. He claimed them, and vaunted finely.

An idea striking Big Man just then, he pointed to me, and said:

"Can put him down?"

"Just as easy as I can turn my hand over." And Joe elevated his nose, as if I were a very contemptible antagonist.

"You can't do it, Joe," said I, stung by his contempt.

"Come out here," he said.

I stepped out. Joe laid his right hand on my left shoulder, and gave me a jerk, accompanied by a quick trip on the left heel. But I had not been ten years, summer and winter, to a district school, for nothing. I was moderately expert at "rough and tumble," and though Joe followed up his first trip by others quicker and more furious, I found no difficulty in shoring myself up. My arms were longer than his, and I thrust him back so far that he found difficulty in tripping. Then I assumed the offensive, and tried in many ways to upset him, but I could not.

Our struggles were too exhausting to last long. Making two legs answer for half a dozen, and my offensive movements, soon put me out of breath. And Joe's unremitted exertions had winded him. So, as if by mutual agreement, we separated.

All this was sport for the Kanakas. They laughed and chattered like magpies, and when Joe drew back, puffing, they asked him—

"Where your smart? You no put him down. Where your brag?"

After that day, whenever Joe could find me out of sight of the officers, he would clinch me. In these encounters his aim was to close with me, and mine was to prevent him. For some time, therefore, there was no decisive struggle. At length, he got inside of my arms, and took a back hold. Down I went! Joe began to exult. My best "hold" at wrestling was at what we used to call "side hold" at school. I offered battle again. Joe rushed in, but before he could get a grasp behind me, I whirled around, bringing him on my right side. As I whirled, I passed my right arm around his waist, and grasped his right hand with my left. I was all right then, and before Mr. Bacon saw through it, he was upon his back on the deck, and I was lying across his breast. So we were square. And we kept about square thereafter.

One day my father surprised us in the midst of a furious heat. We received a short and impressive lecture, such as only seafaring men can give, and I was particularly warned never to be caught wrestling again. It was very hard for Joe to abstain. For sometime after, whenever he met me his arms were involuntarily stretched out towards me.

October 6th we crossed the Equator again, and were once more in the Northern Hemisphere. We now experienced a great deal of unpleasant weather. One afternoon the wind began to blow hard from the N. E. We took in one sail after another, until nothing was left on the ship but the close reefed topsails, reefed foresail, main spencer, and fore-topsail staysail. We were on a wind, lying as near it as we could.

Just after it became dark a furious squall struck us, accompanied by torrents of rain. The ship went down upon her broadside fearfully, almost upon her beam ends. After infinite labor we got the topsails clewed up, the foresail hauled up, and the staysail hauled down.

The Kanakas were almost useless. In the intense darkness they could not find the ropes, and they seemed paralyzed by the unparalleled roar of the tempest. When we went aloft to furl the topsails, they went with us, but neither persuasion nor blows could induce them to get upon the yards. They clung in the rigging, indifferent to all that was said or done to them.

I shall never forget the toil, and the consequent exhaustion of that night. When at length, no more could be done towards making the ship snug, we dragged ourselves, with limbs trembling with fatigue, to our respective stations. This gale abated the next day. The incompetency exhibited by the Kanakas made us dread the occurrence of the next.

An accident befell Big Man one day. At the foot of the forecastle steps was a hatchway opening into the lower hold. For some purpose the steps were removed, and this hatchway opened. Big Man came from the wheel, and not knowing what had been done, and without looking before him, began to descend into the forecastle as if the steps were there. He fell, of course, and in falling he contrived to turn heels up, and go through the hatchway below head foremost. On the keelson, just under this hatchway, the kedge anchor was lying, and about it quite a number of sacks of coarse salt. As he came down, Big Man's head struck fairly on the shank of the anchor, and his body bumped down upon the sacks of salt. How far were his brains scattered? the reader may ask.

He was a man weighing three hundred pounds, and he had fallen twenty feet without hindrance, and had alighted head foremost on the shank of an anchor. The inquiry is pertinent—How far were his brains scattered?

If he had any, they were undisturbed. His sole hurt was a piece of scalp knocked off!

Now, in the name of common sense, of what was the skull composed that withstood such a shock? If of common material, how thick was it?

Again my mind reverted to my Kanaka on the hill behind Honolulu. Fancy should play me no more such tricks, I resolved. In what way would a mere thirty-two pound cannon ball, dashed by a human hand, harm the head of a Kanaka?

How invaluable is experience!

CHAPTER XXIV.

WHIRLWINDS.—THE MONKEYS PERFORM.—THE HOOGLY.—CALCUTTA AT LAST.

ONE whole season, as we measure time here in our temperate zone, had passed since we left Honolulu, we were in the middle of a second, and still our destination was distant. The weather was very fretful, and the safety of the ship required unremitting vigilance on the part of the officers.

We thought one day, even after the Bay of Bengal was no longer remote, that we should never sail upon its waters, and that our prolonged voyage would suddenly end in the quiet of the ocean's depths.

A chaffing, vexing, wearying morning had succeeded a laborious night. The varying wind, unsteady in force and direction, had brought us to close reefs, and then died away. While we waited, grimly watching the leaden sky and blank horizon, roaring, shrieking, and whistling sounds arose ahead of us, astern of us, on the right hand and on the left. And in as many directions, and more, not far off, the water became agitated. It rose and fell like water boiling over a fire. It foamed, and a thick mist went up from it. Then the water itself rose slowly up—rose as the potter's clay rises—and the hand of the fierce whirlwind shaped it. From the peaked tops the great drops rained off like drops from a whirling water-wheel. These creations, receiving the power of motion, began to traverse the sea. Some moved towards us—some went from us. They performed a kind of solemn dance, approaching each other and retiring again, and swaying measuredly from side to side. It was a superstition among the Arabs that whirlwinds on the desert, and whirlwinds and waterspouts on the sea were caused by swift motions of the evil Genii. It was easy to conceive of these objects about us as gigantic Jinnees dancing to appropriate music, which they themselves furnished. *Gigantic* Jinnees, I say, for these flexible columns of water were, in height, from thirty to fifty feet. We stood watching the approaching monsters, anticipating destruction, but giving it no thought. Escape seemed impossible; the ship was motionless—there was not a breath of wind to fill the little sail that was spread.

But our time was not come. One that had been slowly approaching on our larboard beam—one that we expected would fall upon us and rend us to shreds, hurling our spars aloft as an angry child hurls jackstraws—that one an Unseen Hand turned aside, and it went roaring by our bow. Another at the same time, was moving down upon our starboard quarter. There seemed no possibility of escape. Indeed, we had no hope. But the Unseen Hand was again stretched out. A puff of wind struck us on the starboard bow, and the ship wore slowly round and moved away.

The whirlwind, having in its embrace the writhing column of water, passed by our stern, then bent around on a course parallel to ours, and moved past us, for our breath of wind had died away.

There was a fascination in this scene which it is impossible to describe. I think we must have felt as those feel who are charmed by serpents. The appalling danger—just as apparent as it could be—was more than balanced by the awful charm of its appearing.

These water-sprites did not disfigure the sea long. Their proportions grew more and more shrunken, and in less than half an hour from their birth, they were drowned in a torrent of rain.

Once in the Bay of Bengal, we saw vessels frequently. Now and then a Bengal junk went by, exciting our mirth by her grotesque appearance.

Occasionally we had exhibitions of turtles. Two monstrous fellows were discovered close alongside one day. The appearance of the ship seemed to frighten them, and they set all their locomotive powers in hurried motion. It was not strange that Paddy, on seeing the head, legs, and other members of a turtle struggling beneath the rim of his shell, exclaimed, " Arrah, here's a box full of snakes!"

Our monkeys were very mischievous. They carried things hither and thither, and it was very difficult to find them when wanted.

When we drew near the head of the Bay, the deep sea lead and line were brought up, to be prepared for accurate sounding. In order to do this, a space of a certain number of fathoms in extent was measured off on one side of the main deck, the extremities chalked off, and the line stretched from one to the other.

All these movements the monkeys watched with breathless interest, from the main hatch. Suddenly they all disappeared. Having occasion, a few minutes afterwards, to cross to the other side of the deck, to my great amazement I found them imitating our movements as nearly as they could—and the imitation was very good, I assure you.

They had been around forward of the house and stolen our chalk, and into the house and stolen a ball of cotton twine. Their space on the deck—about equal to ours—had already been measured and chalked; and when I came upon them, one sat by the after mark holding the end of the twine, while another was going forward with the ball, unwinding as he went. The others sat by the forward mark, looking as grave and wise as owls.

I drew back and told what was going on, and all crossed over to witness the performance. But it seemed that the monkeys could not abide spectators. Finding themselves observed, they left their job in a poor state of completion, and ran off.

It is recorded that there have been people who believed that monkeys could both speak and understand human language, but would not exercise their gifts for fear of being set to work. If that is the case, they are not very observing, else they would see that among men, those who talk most work least. "*Great talkers, little doers,*" you know.

October 20th we reached green water, and found bottom with the lead. We had reached the Sand Heads. After beating about for a day or two in the vicinity of Point Palmiras and Balasora Roads, we reached the Floating Light, and got a pilot.

The land about the mouth of the Hoogly is very low and even. When making it we saw first the trees which grow along the shore—or, I should say, the branches of the trees, for the branches were visible before the trunks, and had the appearance of being suspended in the air. By-and-by the low bank came to view, and finally the trunks of the trees, linking the land and branches together.

I pass over the names of localities, some of which were peculiar and profane, and over the stories of the pilot about wrecks, quicksands, tigers and alligators.

From the mouth of the river to the city the distance is about one hundred miles. When about half way up, I climbed up on the main royal yard and took a look about. The low land lay as level as the sea on a calm day. In some places there was a thick undergrowth of shrubs, but not an elevation of land anywhere in view that amounted to a knoll. The jackals howled hideously through the nights. Often by day we could see them on the shore, contending with the buzzards for some coveted bit of carrion. They must have been very numerous on the banks of the river, judging from the noise they made in their nightly concerts.

As we drew near the city we met, frequently, the great, awkward river boats descending. Finally we arrived safely at our destination, and the ship was moored off one of the ghauts or landing places of the city. Many vessels lay in the stream, discharging or receiving cargo.

We had not been long moored before a milkman made his appearance, and offered to furnish us with milk during our stay. He brought a sample of his milk with him to be tested, which, on trial, was found very good. So on his next visit he was encouraged to make a business of coming. A Sabbath occurring soon, I purchased on my own account, a quart of the lacteal fluid from him, that I might enjoy to my heart's content—stomach's capacity—a favorite dish, hard bread and milk. As soon as the milk was poured out, I filled a bowl and broke in the bread, and then left it to soak a little while. When sufficient time had elapsed I returned to the pantry, my mouth watering, and anticipating a feast. There seemed to be a lack of milk in the bowl, the bread having absorbed it, and I took up the pitcher to supply the deficiency. But when I looked into it I found it filled with whitish water. I tipped it, and saw a chalky sediment at the bottom. I shook it, and it assumed its old appearance of milk. And this mixture was to pass muster for milk, generous, rich, life-giving milk!

I submitted the contents of the pitcher to the inspection of the higher powers, and threw the mess in the bowl overboard. When our smooth-faced, white-robed milkman mounted the side the next morning, he was immediately kicked out through an open port into his dinghy, and there was an end of that speculation.

Subsequently we engaged another man to supply milk for our coffee, morning and noon-time. He furnished a passable, if not a pure article. I had my hard bread and milk several times, but I could never make it come up to the home standard.

A very few days at Calcutta convinced me that it was not a place for me to thrive in. The atmosphere seemed to oppress me, and I was conscious that I grew weaker daily.

A gang of Lascars, under the direction of a chief or foreman (I have forgotten his local title), were engaged to do duty on board. A number of these foremen came on board to get employment for themselves and their gangs. They brought with them, and exhibited with great confidence, recommendations from the various captains whom they had served. They could not read English, and on that account some of the documents which they presented for recommendations did not contain much to their credit.

The one whom my father engaged offered as a recommendation a paper from an English captain, which certified that the bearer was a "great cheat, rascal, liar, and knave generally."

What consideration led him to accept the services of such a character, I cannot imagine, unless it was this: He *might* be disappointed in any one whom he engaged. In this one he could only be *agreeably* disappointed.

We had some pigs on board, and they often had the privilege of walking the main deck. It was amusing to us to see how fearful our Lascars were of coming in contact with them. Your true Hindoo, even of the Soodra caste, abominates swine as much as your Jew, or Mussulman.

Many a horrid look have I brought upon myself, many a hearty Hindoo curse, and many a threat of blood-letting by the handy sheath-knife, upon which the hand was laid, and all because I drove the pigs among them. I had no idea then that I was running any risk, but now I really believe that had I driven a grunter against one of those bigoted, superstitious, idolatrous, heathen wretches, he would have run his sheath-knife into me with a superlatively pious fury.

These people did not possess much physical strength. And for that matter, how could they? Their whole subsistence was rice and curry, and they did not eat as much of that in one day as I should require (barring the curry, of which more hereafter,) for a luncheon.

While they were employed on board the casks of nails and spikes, to which I have before referred, were discharged to make room for the coming cargo. They performed a part of the labor, and it was while they were about it that I noticed how weak they were. It was only by the greatest exertion that one of them could tip a cask of nails from its bilge upon its head. My brother, who was carrying on the work, would get out of all patience with them, and, as an example for them to emulate, would catch up a cask, and tossing it as high as his head, catch it again as it fell. They took it all as a matter of course, however, and seemed to be well aware of the superior strength of Europeans and Americans. Yes, and of Kanakas too; for Big Man would now and then show them something worth regarding.

When they hoisted in concert they had their accompaniment of song. As many of them as could get about a fall or rope, would seize hold of it, and when the signal was given to hoist, one would lead off something after this sort:

"*Jenny Skinner.*"

This brief stanza of one line was, after a proper interval, followed by a chorus as brief, all ejaculating in concert—

"*Hayiyah,*"

and settling away upon the fall

Leader—"*Copell Pitchell.*"

All—"*Hayiyah.*" (Pull.)

Leader—"*Grando Pegrum.*"

All—"*Hayiyah.*" (Pull.) Etc.

But what shall I say of the appearance of the city, and what of the appearance of the sacred river, the principal outlet of the most sacred Ganges? Some, who have been disgusted by my prolixity in former chapters, will anticipate something very long drawn here. They will find me brief, however. I learned but little, comparatively, of the city and river, and I shall not exceed what I beheld and knew. This is a veritable narrative, whatever its merits may be in other respects.

Come with me and behold the river Hoogly. Let us take a position here at the break of the poop, and observe it attentively. Look up towards its source.

Does it come from far?

It is formed by a junction of the Cossimbazar and Jellinghy rivers, the western branches of the Ganges, and the distance from here to that junction is fifty-five miles. You can see that it is a respectable river for width. From "Old Fort Ghaut," here on our right, across to Howra, is a mile, almost. Its waters are decently deep, also, though you don't see that, for it is rather thick and muddy. There are more rapid rivers, but you may know from the strain on the cables of the shipping that the waters of the Hoogly do not stand still.

What is that object up the river yonder, floating down with the current?

Let us wait until the current brings it nearer to us.

Why, it looks like a drowned man!

It *is* the body of a human being—dead, though not drowned; a naked, swollen, putrid human body. And see that crow light on it, and peck at the protruding, staring eyeballs. Horrid! horrid!

But we cannot rid ourselves of the disagreeable impression by turning away our eyes. Similar objects are seen in all directions. There, towards the western shore, swimming deep, and preyed upon by three crows, is another bloated body. Here are two more in the direction of the landing, and more are coming in sight far up. High feasts these afford for the jackals and buzzards!

Plentiful as these bodies appear to be, they are few when the present is compared with earlier times. The English, since they acquired power in the land, have labored, and with some success, to abolish the barbarous custom of the natives, which consigns so many bodies to the waters of the river.

CHAPTER XXV.

AT CALCUTTA.—CURRY.—EXEUNT THE KANAKAS.—
EXPERIENCE AND OBSERVATION.

CALCUTTA is called the "City of Palaces." It is also, more inelegantly, termed the "City of Mud Huts." Looking at it from the river, one saw the justice of both names. From Fort William and the esplanade, far up, stretched a long line of most palatial buildings, right lordly dwellings. But as the eye surveyed them, it fell also on numerous miserable mud huts. In the same degree that the former were lofty and dignified piles, the latter were low and mean habitations.

On the occasion of my first visit to the shore, my father took me along with him. We went first to the places of business of several merchants, and then to the office of the American consul.

At this place I saw a very ingenious device for "raising the wind." The partition wall at one end of the room constituted a gigantic fan. It moved on hinges at the top, and when swung vigorously, as was the case then, got up a fine circulation in the apartment.

We dined with the Consul. There were other guests, one English, and several American captains. The dinner was East Indian—chickens, rice, etc., and the everlasting *curry*.

My curse upon curry! I had never tasted it before. I saw the others convey it to their mouths in considerable quantities, and swallow it with apparent relish. I supposed that I could, and should, do the same. So, with all the rashness with which a boy attacks a new and apparently dainty article of diet, I put a quantity in my mouth, overlooking for the moment, that it was a condiment, and not to be taken by the mouthful. Fire is not hotter than was that mouthful of curry. In that company I could not indulge myself in spitting it out, and howling in my anguish, as I was almost irresistibly impelled to do. Therefore I swallowed it as rapidly as I could, and sent with it and poured after it, a large goblet of ice water. I curled my toes in my agony. I opened my mouth and inhaled the outer air. Better the fox of the Spartan youth, gnawing at the vitals, than the fire of that accursed compound, searing throat and chest. The tears started from my eyes and coursed down my cheeks. And all the time I covered my distress by an appearance of interest in what was transpiring before me.

Curry is a conglomeration, consisting of tumeric, onions, coriander, mustard, black pepper, melted butter, fenugreek, cocoa nut milk, ginger, cummin seed, mushroom powder, ground rice, cayenne pepper, cardamons, etc. There's a list for you!

The elders—*i. e.*, all but myself—at this repast, talked politics, or boasted of their individual deeds. I could not but notice that John Bull eclipsed all others in the latter thing. Drinking and smoking succeeded eating. The talking, as a matter of course, increased. There was now, however, one silent individual besides myself. One American captain, a young man, said nothing, but occupied the time in vainly trying to stand two cigars upon their ends and lay a third one across on top. He could set two upon their ends, but when the third one was laid upon them they all fell down. From the Consul's we returned directly to the ship.

The California passengers had left a great many empty bottles on board. Some may be curious to know what they contained when full, for no one can suppose they brought them on board empty. It was neither water nor milk—so in guessing (for I shall not tell what was in them), do not guess either of those things. These bottles I had collected together, and now I bartered them for oranges. They procured me quite a supply.

I have already said that the air of Calcutta did not agree with me. At the time when I possessed myself of the oranges I was much debilitated. I suffered no pain of any consequence, but grew weaker every day. In order to favor my illness, and at the same time to make me useful, I was directed to middle-stitch the topgallant sails. When sails are made, the breadths of canvass are lapped when they are sewed together. To middle-stitch a sail is to run a thread through the middle of the parts that lap over. The effect is to strengthen the seam.

The topgallant sails were lying with the other sails on the deck in the forward cabin. This was in the shade, of course, and by opening all the doors and windows I secured a cooling current of air. Here I would sit, with some of my oranges about me, and sew. When tired I would lie back upon the sails and rest, or sit up and indulge in an orange or two. After a while Joe Bacon, having become partially disabled, was joined with me in the duty of middle-stitching.

We really enjoyed ourselves, talking, eating oranges, and working *very cautiously*. One day our tête-à-tête was interrupted by an angry altercation not far off. Two individuals no less renowned than Doctor Henry Brown, and his worthy coadjutor, John Gilpin, were at loggerheads. It was plain enough that the Doctor had been imbibing some of his favorite gin, and something had also strangely loosened the tongue of John.

" Jes' tell me," roared the Doctor, in a tone that

at once arrested our attention, "how you 'spect to get 'long board de ship. De capen say you be a fool—nebber make a sailor, an' tell you to help de cook. *Help de cook!* Why, you bodder my soul out."

To these pointed remarks John Gilpin returned a volley of Kanaka gibberish.

"You 'tend to start? I don't cal'late to tolerate dis much more. I show you a new ting. Go light de fire—go light de fire."

Another volley of Kanaka from John, but no movement.

"I tell you jes' dis once—go light de fire!"

Volley, as before.

The disputants stood about three paces apart. The Doctor did not wait for John to finish his reply, but at once laid violent hands on him. It was David assailing Goliath. After some skirmishing, Africa was victorious, and Oceanica was laid upon his back in the passage-way leading out of the cabin. The Doctor who had fallen upon his antagonist, endeavored to rise, but was foiled in this. John now began to make some points, and was like to turn the Doctor under. Joe and I thought it time to go to the rescue. We did not rush, for we were very weak, but we reached the scene of action after a while. Joe grappled into John's hair and held his head down, while I held one of his arms. This must have seemed a good deal like unfair play to John, for he began to shout out a single Kanaka word most lustily. Suspecting that he was calling on the Kanakas in the hold for help, I laid my hand across his mouth to silence him. But he gave my hand a savage bite, and went on with his yelling. It was an amusing struggle. We seemed Lilliputians contending with Gulliver. Having a hand to spare now, the Doctor, who was astride of his foe, picked up a long strip of board that the carpenter had left there a little while before, and struck at John's head again and again. His aim was not good, for he did not hit John at all, but he kept Joe and I dodging pretty sharply. Meantime my father and the custom-house officer, who were walking the deck above, heard the noise, and came down to seek the cause. They came into the cabin just when the Doctor was trying to belabor John's head. As my father came near, the Doctor, who was not aware of his presence, swung back his board for a mighty blow, and gave the captain a smart back-stroke on the side of his head. He seized the stick, and the Doctor, looking around, was greeted with a severe interrogation:

"What's all this?"

The Doctor was noways disconcerted.

"Bery sorry I hit yer, Capen—didn't 'tend for to do it—didn't know yer was about. I axes yer pardon."

"Well, well—but what are you fighting about?"

"Axes yer pardon agin, Capen, but dis ain't fightin'. Dis feller here, John, gib me sass. I show him a new ting. 'Spect he's drunk—mebbe crazy."

Just then up through the hatchway poured all the Kanakas, and at their heels came the mate.

John became silent. His countrymen were also silent. They stood grouped about the hatchway, evidently undecided what to do.

The Doctor got up from sitting astride of John. Joe and I moved to one side. This left John unrestrained, but he did not move. He lay still on his back, glaring at us with eyes as red as fire coals. The captain ordered irons to be put upon his wrists. He submitted to the operation quietly. Then the Kanakas were ordered below again to their work. They went obediently. When the last one had disappeared in the hold the mate turned to the prostrate John, and having kicked him two or three times violently, himself descended into the hold. My father and the officer were already gone. The Doctor was "lightin' de fire" himself. Joe and I, only, witnessed the brutality of the mate.

From our cushion of sails we continued to observe John. All alone, he lay there upon his back, his burning eyes fixed upon the deck above, his wrists bound by the ignominious bracelets. What were his thoughts, poor fellow? Did he regret that he had left his far off lovely Woahoo? Did he accuse his shipmates of cowardice, and the white men of cruelty? Did he still feel the dastardly kicks of the mate? Did he meditate revenge, or was he, after all, in a state of stupefaction?

Before night a policeman came off from the shore and, taking off John's iron handcuffs, replaced them by a brass pair that he took from his pocket. Then he beckoned to the unhappy Kanaka, and they proceeded to the boat, and the boat proceeded to the shore. Never again did I behold John Gilpin.

Miserable Kanaka, it was a hard, and an inexorable fate that dragged thee from the sweet isle of thy nativity, from the sight of its dark mountain peaks, and the shade of its tall cocoa nut trees! Never more shalt thou wet thy tawny skin in the shining surges of the coral reefs, or paddle the outriggered canoe. For thy relishing palate never more shall pig be roasted, or yam, or sweet potatoe, and poi—ah, *poi!* Thou wilt regret that greatest and most appreciated luxury, even shouldst thou sup on ambrosia with thy long-worshipped heathen gods! John died of fever in the city of Calcutta.

My father and the mate had disagreed on the voyage, and they continued to disagree in port. The result was the discharge of the mate. He gathered together his goods, caught his monkey and paroquette, and left us. Shortly after, all the Kanakas, except one, ran off. They received some money and liberty to go on shore, and only one, young John Steward, returned. This defection did not grieve us much.

A new mate was soon shipped, an Englishman named Porter. He had been long in the East Indies, and understood and spoke the language of the people. Also he was an excellent man, and a prime sailor, but being only a man, he could not be faultless—he drank hard.

The second time I went on shore I went early in the morning with this man, Mr. Porter, who, on account of his knowledge of the language and customs, did the marketing. He had, the day before, pitched a waterman out of the ship into his dinghy for some insolence, and the fellow vowed to have revenge. So he took me with him on this particular morning in the capacity of a body guard, as he apprehended the waterman would be on the lookout for him, with some friends to back him up. I was quite weak then, but my large frame made a very good show. It was quite early in the morning, as I have said, and all classes were not astir. As usual, a large number of dinghy-men were collected at the Ghaut, and others were strung all along from thence to the market place. When we were about half way there, Mr. Porter espied his enemy, and pointed him out to me. If angry features and furious glances could kill, we should both have fallen down dead. But they do not, and we came off safely, for he used nothing else against us.

Many people were wending their way to market. Here and there a jackal sneaked away to less frequented streets. Solitary adjutant birds stalked solemnly about. Now and then an officer cantered his horse across the esplanade in the direction of the fort. As soon as our purchases were made, we returned directly to the ship.

The next day the carpenter invited my brother and myself to take a day's cruise on shore with him. He had been making some writing desks of teak, and intended on this occasion to go to the Bazaar to buy brass trimmings for them.

After landing we trudged along the hot, dusty streets, and found but little to interest us until we reached the neighborhood of the Bazaar. Here the scene grew a little more agreeable, and I went forward with a stouter heart. I was really too weak and too much unstrung for all this travel in the hot sun, but I had not taken any extensive walk about the city, and I could not resist the temptation of a stroll with my brother and our great favorite, the carpenter.

We had not been long in the Bazaar before a sharper of a Hindoo, attracted, doubtless, by my verdant appearance, came up to me, and, with a profound salaam, offered to sell me a piece of silk which he said contained eight pocket handkerchief patterns. I asked the price.

"Sixteen rupees—a notable bargain."

He told the truth, and so do all kindred spirits when making similar declarations—notable bargains for *them*.

I assured the man that the article was beyond my means entirely, and walked away. But the silk merchant would not be put off thus. He overtook me, and urged the matter upon me.

"Sahib will do well to examine the texture of the silk. It is of unusual fineness. Such is not often offered to a customer in this city."

I could not do otherwise, I thought, than look at it. My brother and the carpenter joined me. A glance showed this extraordinary piece of goods to be a sham. We told the owner so, and turned our backs upon him. With a pertinacity that would have ranked him high among peddlers in this country, he pursued, and persecuted me for an offer.

"I cannot leave Sahib," he said, "until he has made me an offer."

"Make him a small offer," said the carpenter, "less than he can take; and then, if he don't clear out, kick him."

So I said *three* rupees.

To my infinite surprise the silk was extended to me with a low obeisance, and these words:

"Sahib is a sharp customer. He over-reaches the poor Hindoo."

Didn't he deserve my hat?

Rid of that pest, we went on. While the carpenter was selecting his trimmings, I leaned against a post and scanned the passers by.

Soon a European lady came tripping along—tripping so daintily that, just abreast of me, she tripped in good earnest, and fell over. Before it was evident to my dull perceptions that I ought to step forward and aid he in rising, a smiling, sleek Hindoo, the proprietor of a stall opposite, rushed out, and with most delicate and graceful politeness, assisted the lady up. There was grace and ease in all his motions. He smiled and bowed with such accomplished gallantry to the fair one's repeated acknowledgements, that I beheld him with wonder and admiration.

He stood a moment in the pathway watching the retiring form of the lady, then, turning, cast a glance in the opposite direction. Instantly I saw no common satisfaction leap into his features. He sprang forward again with the same graceful activity which he had displayed while assisting the lady, and which had excited my admiration—to do what? To raise the fresh manure of a cow, and dash it against a wall, to dry for fuel. Bah! Both actions, raising the lady, and *the other*, were exquisitely performed.

Which gave him the liveliest satisfaction, I wonder?

CHAPTER XXVI.

A CHANGE OF MATES AGAIN.—SNAKE CHARMERS AND JUGGLERS.—DEPARTURE FROM CALCUTTA.

HAVE said that Mr. Porter drank hard. He was often "half seas over." At length my father said to him: "Mr. Porter, you must either quit drink, or leave the ship. I like you, but cannot endure your habit of drinking."

"Well," Mr. Porter answered, "we will part friends. I like my berth, but I am not willing to give up liquor."

So Mr. Porter went on shore, regretted by all, for he was a pleasant and cheerful man. And there was a vacancy.

WANTED—A MATE.

A few days afterwards, I was sitting under the awning on the poop deck. A shore boat came alongside, with a white man in the stern. I made a careful survey of him, and internally pronounced him a clergyman, but an unamiable and bigoted one. He came on board, and wished to see the captain. I showed him into the cabin, and then, walking to the stern, lay down upon the transom.

"You want a mate, captain?" said the stranger.

"Yes, sir."

"I would like the situation. I think I can give you satisfaction."

I fairly started. That man a seaman!

"I discharged my last mate," said my father, "because he drank. I want a steady man. Therefore you will excuse me if I ask whether you drink or not."

"I do not, sir. I am strictly temperate."

After a little more conversation, Mr. Jackson—for that was the man's name—was engaged.

About the time that Mr. Jackson joined us, I ceased to do any kind of work. I was very weak; and to walk twice the length of the ship was almost too much exertion for me. I sat most of the time during the day on the poop deck under the awning, and watched, in a listless, uninterested way, the course of events.

The cargo which was brought to the ship presented quite a variety, and was well described as an *assorted* cargo. It consisted of deer's horns, arrack, hides, castor oil, tallow, lac, seeds, etc.

The deck was almost constantly thronged with native laborers. Their almost naked bodies mingled and moved before my eyes, and their din rang in my ears. They were not always nude. Once in a while one would appear in a very original (to me) costume—nothing less than a complete coat of the mud of the Hoogly. It was a source of wonder to me how they contrived to make it adhere so firmly. It did not seem to interfere with the free use of their limbs. One felt in an instant that these were indeed " of the earth earthy."

" Halloo ! "

This prolonged hail would come over the water, followed by the thumping of tom-toms, and the clash of cymbals. Turning my head to seek the cause of all this noise, I would see a large boat drifting down to us with the current. Its occupants, jugglers and snake charmers, would shout—

"Halloo, Sahib, see snakee dance! Very fine snakee."

They would shout the praises of their snakes loudly, as they drifted by.

" We will come on board very quickly," they would add. " We will ask but little money. We will cause to dance very much four very beautiful snakes, and we will show some very fine tricks."

All in vain. No one would have leisure to see the " snakee dance " but myself, and however much I might wish it, I knew they would not be allowed to come on board and disturb the laborers. I would watch the boat as the tide carried it by. When the performers realized that no invitation would be extended to them to come on board, they would gradually cease their vociferations, and finally hush their voices and instruments altogether, and gaze reproachfully at the ship. This silence would denote the death of hope as far as we were concerned.

I would still watch them, as they were borne on by the current. Soon they would turn their eyes from us down stream. Another ship would lie before them. Again I would hear a faint "Halloo," and the distant rub-a-dub of the tom-toms would fall upon my ears. This new burst would denote the revival of hope, and the praises of the snakes would be repeated to other ears. Daily these boats were passing the ship and soliciting patronage.

One Sunday, not long after our arrival, I was, at one hour, the sole occupant of the deck. One of these boats came alongside, and I invited the performers to come on board. In an instant they were upon deck, with their baskets of snakes and bags of utensils. The show began at once. One old fellow opened his bag, and took out what seemed to me to be a common cricket, or footstool, covered with fur, and having a head on one end. This he set on one side, and treated as if it were the genius of jugglery. His first trick I did not comprehend, because of the rapidity with which he performed it. The second was to produce eggs from a bag which he had wrung like a dish-cloth, and beaten upon the deck. All the time he gesticulated

to, he supplicated, he apostrophized his fur-clad idol.
After this trick the music struck up, the snakes were
let out, and the dance began. The reptiles rose
upon their tails and writhed solemnly about.

At this juncture the performance was interrupted.
The music had attracted all hands to the deck. My
father no sooner saw what was going on than he
ordered the performers into their boat immediately.
I threw them what copper coin I had. The snakes
were hurried into their baskets, the magic god was
bagged again, and the deck was clear in a minute.
Before retiring to his cabin the captain positively
forbid the introduction of any more snake-dancers
or jugglers into the ship on Sunday.

During the time we lay here, several religious
holidays occurred. The festivities and ceremonies
consequent upon them enlivened many of my lonely
hours spent under the awning on the poop. The
sounds of the musical instruments filled my ears,
and the flash of tinsel, the waving of banners, and
the swaying of the multitudes, filled my eyes.

It was at the close of these holidays, I believe,
that they cast the gods of the occasion into the
river. All the river above us was filled with boats,
loaded with gaudily dressed people. The shores
were thronged. Gay trappings flaunted in the sun.
The great hosts emitted a hoarse roar, continuous
as the hum from a hive of bees. Above this, at

intervals, rang the musical instruments. Through the day I watched, with wonder and amazement, this scene of oriental magnificence and folly.

My last visit to the shore was made three or four days before our departure. In charge of Mr. Jackson, I went to the Hospital for medical advice. I was able to walk only a few steps. At the landing I got into a palanquin, and was conveyed to my place of destination. There they showed me into a room on the ground floor, and told me to sit down on a long wooden bench. Mr. Jackson then went in pursuit of the doctor. I stretched myself at full length upon the bench, for the jolting of the palanquin had quite exhausted me. As I lay I looked through an open door into a large garden. Some people belonging to the hospital were there, pitching quoits. They were much interested, and had many doubtful points to discuss. Soon the doctor came and prescribed for me, and I was then jolted back to the landing. I cannot say much in praise of the palanquin as a mode of conveyance.

When we reached the ship again there was a stranger in the cabin. I soon learned that he was a Mr. George Christie, a Scotsman, and that he would take passage with us to London. He had been twelve years in the British East Indian army. He and the custom-house officer manifested much sympathy for me. Indeed, the officer had all along been very kind. When I would be particularly low he would say:

"I see, my boy, that you require a little stimulant."

Then he would send on shore for a bottle of port wine. He prided himself on knowing how to give the finest tone to port. He prepared it with spices, and it was really delicious. We shared quite a number of bottles, and I found that it did brace me up, and afford me a temporary vigor. In the end, however, I should probably have been better off without it.

After Mr. Christie came on board the bottles were sent for more frequently. He loved a social glass most dearly—too dearly, we learned afterwards, for his own good. He was a very meritorious soldier, but his unhappy passion for strong drink had been fatal to his promotion, and he left off as he began, a private in Her Majesty's Lances. Under the influence of the genial port his heart opened wide, and he told many fascinating stories of battle, and adventure, in that rich and populous land.

At length the end came. The cargo was all on board, the hatches secured, and a crew shipped. The anchors were hove up out of the mud of the Hoogly, and we began our descent.

My father remained in the city to conclude his

business, as it would be easy to overtake the ship in a river craft.

All was confusion on board. Mr. Jackson, our "strictly temperate" mate, began to give his solemn declaration the lie. He was soon so drunk as to be unable to attend to his duties. My brother, the second mate, with a portion of the crew, were engaged on the rigging. Once in a while Mr. Jackson would rush out from his state-room, and assume the direction of affairs. On one of these occasions he found the men setting up the fore topgallant backstays.

"That will do," said my brother. "Clap on a seizing, and shift the tackle."

"Hold on, hold on!" said Mr. Jackson. "You havn't enough on it by a foot, Mr. D——. Settle away on it, lads, settle away."

The lads did settle away, but the obstinate piece of rigging would not budge another inch. Mr. Jackson called them a set of slimsy swabs, and ordered them to get a snatch-block, and lead the fall to the capstan.

While they were doing this he sought a proper place to note the effect. Finding no place on deck to suit him, he got upon the house and stood upon some wood that lay between the boats. As he threw back his head to look upwards at the topgallant mast, he fell over backwards on the wood, and a splinter, which chanced to be pointing upwards, stuck deeply into his flesh. He wriggled himself up, and, swearing horribly, retired to his state-room. When he was out of sight, my brother directed the men, as before, to clap a seizing on the lanyard, and shift the tackle.

No more was seen of the mate for some time. He appeared again, however, and this time the fore royal stay was on the docket. The men were hauling it taut by hand, for it was not a rope of any great consequence.

"That is no way to set up rigging," said Mr. Jackson. "Put on a watch tackle."

A watch tackle was put on.

"Now, men, away with it! Pull, men, pull!"

The spar bent forward. The topgallant stay grew slack.

"Will not that do, sir?" asked my brother.

"No, no!" replied the mate. I dislike this doing things by halves. Away with it, men—away with it. Have you no strength?"

The men only pretended to pull.

"Jump out there, one of you, with a slush bucket, and give it a greasing."

"That has been done already, sir," said my brother.

"Then go out, one of you, and shake it. It will render better. The rest of you take the fall to the capstan. It's strange that all of you can't set up that stay."

"It will part," said my brother.

"Let it part then. Heave away, men. Walk around with the bars. Shake it up there—shake it up. There, now it comes home beautifully. Always do—"

Snap! went the slender stay just above the boom, nearly throwing the man there off into the water. One end fell with a splash into the river, and the other swung inboard, while the spar jumped back, straightening the topgallant stay out again, and making it quiver like a taut bowstring.

Mr. Jackson, without another word, turned short on his heel and went aft, followed by the jeers of the men. In the evening he became delirious, and talked of jumping overboard. Two or three times he threw his leg over the rail with that intention (he said), but was seized and drawn back again by my brother and the pilot. My father reached the ship during the night. What passed between him and Mr. Jackson I do not know. It was too late then to make another change.

The next day the confusion that had previously reigned, subsided, and the system and regularity that characterize proceedings on ship board began to appear.

The ship proved to be very crank. When an

anchor was let go from one bow, she would roll down two or three streaks the opposite way. The pilot at first declared he should protest against her going to sea in that condition. He gave up the idea, however.

I suspect that the Hoogly is ascended and descended with greater rapidity and ease now, than then. Occasionally we saw a ship towed up or down by steam, but nearly all won their way by wind and current. It was very laborious. There was but little rest from making and taking in sail; from heaving up anchors, and bracing yards about. One by one the remembered objects upon the river were passed, and by-and-by the open sea lay before us. We lay at anchor off Sangor Island, New Year's Day, 1851. It was a calm and beautiful day. The crew were provided with means to "splice the main brace"—a thing that they did heartily—and in the cabin the bottle went round, inspiring a great deal of good fellowship. Our total abstinence mate took his glass.

Did he or the captain remember a conversation held in that same cabin a few weeks before, on the subject of temperate mates? I did.

The next day the pilot was discharged, and we went to sea.

I began to recruit immediately. When ten days out I was able to do light work. I have wondered what thus lifted me from helplessness, and the point of death almost, in so short a time, to comparative health. Was it the doctor's pills, or the port wine, or the change from the air of Calcutta to that of the wide ocean?

One Kanaka, young John Steward, remained on board. Our new men were British subjects, mostly Scotch, and were all active, able seamen.

We had very good weather through the months of January and February. The crankness of the ship interfered very much with her progress. She behaved better at sea, however, than in the river. This was owing to the greater buoyancy possessed by salt water. But in salt water, or in fresh, she would be down on her broadside when the wind was any other way than aft. When other vessels would be carrying topgallant sails on the wind, we would be crawling along under double reefed topsails, almost on our beam ends, and sliding to leeward about as fast as we moved ahead. This crankness was, in great measure, owing to the manner in which the cargo was stowed. The lighter kinds were in the bottom of the hold. The result of this stowage was foreseen, but it could not be helped. It was necessary to stow the cargo as it was delivered, and, unfortunately, the lighter kinds were delivered first.

February 17th the southern end of Madagascar

bore north, distant 175 miles. March 3d we encountered a violent gale. We were then on the bank of Lagullas, which, six or seven hundred feet under the sea, is the first step of a gigantic series, reaching from the bottom of the Southern Ocean to the high table lands of Africa. Cape Lagullas, the most southerly point of Africa, bore N. N. W., distant 120 miles. Generally we call passing to the southward of the African peninsula, rounding the Cape of Good Hope. And in the minds of most people, the Cape of Good Hope is the most southerly point of Africa.

How much this is an error may be seen from the following statement of latitudes. Cape of Good Hope, south latitude 34° 22'—Cape Lagullas, south latitude 34° 51'. Cape Lagullas is therefore twenty-nine miles farther to the south than the Cape of Good Hope.

CHAPTER XXVII.

WE PASS THE CAPE OF GOOD HOPE.—ST. HELENA.—
A SQUALL.—MAKE THE EDDYSTONE LIGHT.

THE gale of the third of March was purely a tempest of wind. The sky was cloudless, and the sun bright. The ship was hove to with her head to the westward. There was a fearful sea —the worst we encountered during the whole voyage.

I was accustomed to take meridian observations of the sun with an old quadrant that I had, and afterwards work out the latitude. When we brought up our instruments that day to take meridian observations, it was amusing to see what positions the observers took in order to stand still. I got astride of the spanker boom, and with one foot on the top of a skylight and the other hugged to the spar, watched the great orb across the meridian.

Three or four ships, also lying to, were in sight to windward of us.

The next day the gale abated. Meantime we had surged in considerably towards the land. We even fancied we saw the loom of the mountains. I assert that our fancies were not deceitful, for, if that was not Africa, I never saw it, and that I do not wish to confess.

Cape Horn lies in south latitude 55° 59'. The Cape of Good Hope, as I stated in the last chapter, lies far up on a comparatively summer region. Both names were once names of terror to the mariner. The *Cabo Tormentoso* (Cape of Storms), of Bartholemew Diaz, was not immediately forgotten under the more inspiring name of Cape of Good Hope, though until the new era in navigation, it seems to have been regarded as less formidable than Cape Horn. Twenty years ago the latter name was suggestive of nothing but frowning skies, and fierce wrestling with the Storm King. At present, while either is held to be preferable to Cape Cod, in winter, the Cape of Good Hope is considered the worse of the two. The sea is heavier. Not a few ships have gone down to bilge on the bank of Lagullas.

There is an essential difference between lying to in a gale off the Cape of Good Hope, and what immediately succeeds to it in a ship bound to the westward, viz., "rolling down to St. Helena."

After reaching the Atlantic, we struck the S. E. trade winds, and laid our course for the Rocky Isle. The sea was regular and gentle, the wind steady, and the air exhilarating. The yards were laid square. Studding sails were set alow and aloft, on both sides. The sea and the sky were of the same glorious blue.

What nights for "yarning and calking." What days for cleaning ship!

The running rigging was cast off from the pins and stoppered. Bulwarks were scrubbed and painted. Astern lines were trailing for dolphins (Coryphene). The "watch below" haunted the martingale with the harpoon and grains.

Ah! there was poetry and pleasure, and a delicious dreaminess in those days! No path in life is utterly laborious and cheerless. Mariners, you see, are not always tempest-tossed. They have their halcyon days.

Mr. Christie, after so long a time spent amid turbulent and exciting scenes, enjoyed exceedingly the incomparable days and lovely nights, that came and went like pleasant dreams. Mr. Jackson, even, grew grimly genial, and related, as positive facts, scores of impossible and outrageous lies.

March 18th we beheld, far ahead, St. Helena projecting out of the water like a dark cloud. Approaching nearer, we saw, along the water line, the waves driven against the precipitous shore, and above, high, irregular hills, ravines, and elevated plateaus; and we confessed that St. Helena was not indebted to association alone, for power to interest and impress a beholder. I did not think then, that this had been the prison of Napoleon, but the spectacle—the sublime spectacle—of that narrow, but lofty isle, rearing itself out of the blue, fathomless sea, so firm, so unshaken, putting aside the mightiest and angriest billows, moved me, young and untaught as I was. All feel this subduing power. The traveller bares his head in the presence of Niagara—phrases of admiration are not spoken at the feet of the Alps.

Before sunset we had rounded the northern end of the island, and anchored off Jamestown, on the north-west, or leeward side. Many vessels were lying at anchor. We came to, near an American whale ship, the Corinthian.

A black clipper brig, with only the bare lower masts standing, and so light as to preclude the idea of ballast, lay close in to the shore, just to the right hand of the shipping. On the shore near her were two hulks, one of which was partly cut to pieces. These three had been slavers. They had been captured on the African coast, and taken to St. Helena, and condemned. They were now meeting an unusual fate. Most ships, at their final dissolution, are submerged in the sea. These, on the contrary, were broken up and used for fuel.

Jamestown is situated in a ravine. Ladder Hill

and High Knoll lie on the right, and form a *two story* mountain. Ladder Hill is the first story—High Knoll the second. To the top of High Knoll the distance is about 2,000 feet.

Jamestown consists of one principal street, about a mile in length. A mountain stream flows through the place, supplying the inhabitants and shipping with pure and excellent water.

Fortifications abounded. They were the first works of art that met my eyes in approaching the place—upon them my glances rested oftenest while there, and they were the last to grow indistinct in the gloom when we sailed away.

To the left of the town, looking from the shipping, the military men had effected lodgements midway in the high cliffs, and established batteries there. Ladder Hill, up which there is a *ladder*, composed of 675 steps, is crowned by a fortress; and High Knoll, the second story, bears aloft still another.

A kind of small mackerel were very plentiful here. Canoes were all about among the shipping, whose owners caught and sold these fish. Their manner of taking them was new to us. They used, instead of one hook, a bundle. They were tied firmly together, with the points all outward. Just above the shanks of the hook was attached a showy bait to attract the mackerel. When this *aggregate* hook was lowered into the water, the fish would gather thickly about the bait. Then the fisherman would suddenly jerk up on his line, and impale a number upon the projecting points.

A man came alongside our ship in his canoe, and wished to sell some fish. With his permission, I fished a little with his *manifold* jig. I had quite good success, for great skill was not required to handle it properly. These mackerel, when cooked, seemed delicious to our salt beef tempered palates.

Our water was filled from a water boat. It was of an excellent quality. Wood is a very scarce article at St. Helena. All we could purchase for fuel had once sailed the sea as plank and timber of a slaver. It was easy, however, to procure supplies of fresh meat and vegetables.

On board of our neighbor, the Corinthian, were two ladies—one the captain's wife. Their hats and shawls were observed by me with great delight, when they appeared upon the quarter deck of the whaler. They gave the old blubber-hunter a Christian and home-like look.

I did not go on shore, and therefore, have nothing to relate, either concerning Longwood, the residence of Napoleon, or of his Tomb. I feel that it was a misfortune to me, and I lament it—but let no one else lament it.

Descriptions of these localities abound—minute ones, for those who love particulars—precise ones, for those who love exactness—and amusing ones for those who desire a little humor to season dry details.

The Island of St. Helena was discovered on St. Helena's Day, May 21, 1501, by Juan de Nova Castella, a navigator in the service of Portugal. Consequently, the Portugese first possessed it. Then the Dutch got possession of it—then the English—then the Dutch again—and so it went, like a shuttlecock, back and forth, for some time, between the Dutch and English, until it finally settled (as many other places have), into the hands of the English.

There are found upon it pretty conclusive evidences of its volcanic origin. Diana's Peak, the highest part, is 2,700 feet above the level of the sea. The shape of the Island is a compromise between round and square. The greatest distance across it is ten miles and a half. Its area is forty-seven square miles. It lies in south latitude 15° 57′. The distance to the nearest point of Africa is 1,400 miles—to the nearest point of South America 2,000 miles.

We were at St. Helena but two days. We sailed just as the sun was setting, and the Corinthian sailed in company. We packed on everything, alow and aloft, and the island soon disappeared in the gloom. Next morning the Corinthian was two or three miles ahead. She was a very fast sailer. At ten o'clock she lay by for us to come up. We passed close by her stern. My father lifted his hat to the ladies, to whom he had been introduced, exchanged a few words with the captain, and then we were out of hearing. Having thus said goodbye, the whaleman filled away again. He steered more to the westward than we did, and at night was hull down. We pursued our solitary way. Ascension was visible when we passed its latitude, but it was very dim and distant.

When we drew near the Equator the trade wind began to fail us. A short calm succeeded, then a succession of light winds from all points of the compass. All of one afternoon the wind held from the south. The studding sails were run up on both sides in order to get as much distance as we could out of it. Before night, however, it began to change. First it was south-east, then east, then north-east. The studding sails were hauled down, and the yards gradually braced forward. At length the wind came from north. Still we did not rig in the studding-sail boom, or unreeve the studding-sail gear, because it was possible the wind might continue to change, and give us a chance to set the sails again. But by four o'clock the succeeding morning there was no further change, save that the sky grew darker at the north. At that hour the starboard watch went below, and the larboard came on deck. My father, who had been up most of the night, directed Mr. Jackson, if the wind did not change within an hour, to unreeve the studding-sail gear, rig in the booms, and furl the light sails. He then went below and lay down in his cot.

I awoke in the morning just as the grey dawn was stealing into the cabin windows. Not a sound could be heard, or a motion felt. I lay still awhile. A bed feels good in the morning, on board a ship, as well as on shore.

By-and-by I heard my father jump out of his cot, and I knew by his movements that he was consulting the barometer, which hung in the skylight. After a smothered exclamation or two, he seemed to be hastily putting on his pants. I sprang out, and pulled on mine. Then he hurried to the deck, and I followed close behind. As I passed the barometer, I gave it a flying look, and saw, as I had suspected, that it had fallen alarmingly. When we reached the deck, which was pretty quickly, Mr. Jackson was moving from aft, rubbing his eyes, and not yet half awake. A glance aloft showed that he had neglected his orders. The studding-sail booms were out, the gear all rove, and all sail set, from the flying jib to the spanker—from the royals to the deck. And just to windward, close aboard, was a furious squall bearing down upon us. Before it, on the water, went a line of white foam. Above this was a black, perpendicular, impenetrable wall, reaching to the frantically flying clouds.

"Go below, sir!" said my father to Mr. Jackson. "Go directly below, sir. Hard up your wheel—work sharp! Call all hands. Clew up royals and topgallant sails, fore and aft. Down flying jib and staysails. Brail up the spanker——"

I heard no more, for I had clewed up the mizzen royal, and was on my way up to furl it.

The ship was falling off rapidly, and I felt certain she would have her stern presented to the squall when it struck. As I gained the topmast crosstrees, the topgallant yard settled away. With all the activity I was master of I clambered along. I had just got the little pocket handkerchief thing gathered up, when the squall struck. The topgallant sail swelled out and threshed. At every flop the mast jumped back and forth in a way that made it difficult for me to hold on. I twisted one leg about the backstay, and then, feeling secure, went to work. Both arms were employed in keeping the sail in the furl, and the great difficulty was to get hold of the bunt gasket. This I did after a while, and then the rest of the furling was easily accomplished. In my descent I aided in furling the topgallant sail.

When I had reached the deck, the ship was beginning to come to the wind again, and I heard the order given to settle away the fore and mizzen topsails for reefing. It was at a great expense of labor, and not until after some time had elapsed, that all things were put to rights. Then the old ship, with her head about W. N. W., and away down on her broadside, clawed to windward what she could.

Mr. Jackson was off on duty. With his accustomed disregard for truth, he denied that he had slept upon his watch. And as to the studding-sail booms and gear, he said he was about to see to it all. He had not deemed the squall, which he had been watching all the time, was so near.

The man at the wheel, however, declared that Mr. Jackson had been sleeping, and moreover, (this he added privately to me,) he might have slept until the ship herself fell overboard, before he would have roused him. Evidently this man did not admire the worthy Mr. J.

April 1st we crossed the equinoctial line for the sixth and last time. Shortly after, we crossed our old track from Bath to San Francisco. This was indubitable proof that the earth is round.

Again we saw the Sargasso Sea, and its floating

islands of matted weeds. This was an indication that we were approaching our native land again.

Mr. Jackson, having promised better fashions, was reinstated in his office. We passed in sight of the Azores, and while they were yet in view, the wind died away. An English brig, bound to the south, was also becalmed within a mile of us. Supposing that she was not long out, our boat was lowered, and Mr. Jackson boarded her to learn the news. He returned with a bushel of potatoes, and a bundle of newspapers. From these papers we learned of the Crystal Palace at London, and how high expectation was in regard to it.

"Good!" we exclaimed to each other. "We shall be there (at London) at just the right time."

After a few more days we reached the Channel, and closed in with the land. The sun went down, but no England was visible, much to our disappointment. In the evening, however, some one, having mounted the rigging, discovered a light. We conjectured from its bearing that it was the Eddystone Light. In an hour it was plainly to be seen from deck. About midnight an English brig, bound out, shoved along by our quarter.

After the usual hailing, my father made some special inquiries.

"What Light is this in sight?"

"The *Heddystone*."

"So I supposed. What time of tide is it?"

"'*I*gh water."

"Thank you."

And the cockney craft slowly disappeared.

CHAPTER XXVIII.

ARRIVE AT LONDON.—SAIL FOR HOME.—GRAVESEND.
—ARRIVE AT BOSTON.—CONCLUSION.

THE wind blew down channel, and our progress was very slow. Back and forth, back and forth, we went, between the Bill of Portland and Cape La Hague. At this time Mr. Jackson was guilty of another breach of duty, and was again sent below. We were entirely out of fuel, and nearly out of provisions; and when a Portsmouth pilot hailed us, off the Isle of Wight, he was engaged to take the ship into Portsmouth, and soon thereafter we were lying at anchor off Ryde.

Having refitted, we again put out, and now found the wind more favorable. Beachy Head, Dungeness, and the Cliffs of Dover were passed, and at night we anchored in Margate Roads. The next morning a steamer took us in tow, and we got on at a more satisfactory rate.

At Gravesend we anchored to receive a visit from the custom-house officials. My father took passage on a river steamer, and proceeded forthwith to London.

In the afternoon, an officer, with a gang of men and the necessary instruments, came off to see that the revenue of Great Britain received no detriment from us. They pried into everything, and probed and sounded, as if they were medical men called to examine the old ship's lungs. In searching my chest for contraband articles, they discovered my wonderful silk handkerchief bargain. This silk, by the way, was *not* silk, but the fibre of bamboo. During the passage I had cut the patterns apart, and hemmed them all. This, I had been told by the sailors, would save them from being sealed up by the custom house men on our arrival. Now this revenue man who had boarded us took a different view of the matter. He told me to select as many as I wished to use in port, and the remainder he would seal up. I laid my hand upon the whole.

"Impossible," said he. "Four are as many as you need."

A spirit of contradiction entered into me.

"Sir," I said, "the whole eight pieces are not four handkerchiefs. See," and I placed two of the flimsy things together—"you wouldn't dare to blow your nose *hard* on these two together."

"Select four," he said, in a very cross tone; we have no time to talk."

I became angry and saucy. "Do you fear I'll sell them? Do you think your countrymen fools enough to buy such stuff? Green as I am, I—"

He did not wait to hear any more of my harangue, but taking up four of the disputed rags, carried them off out of the state room. I went on deck in a rage, where I tramped about grandly on the high-heeled boots of my passion. Pretty soon one of the revenue men called me below. The officer himself was standing in the forward cabin with a bundle by him which had been opened. He called my attention to it. I saw a small silk shawl, several silk handkerchiefs, and a few other things which I am now unable to mention. The whole had been wrapped up in a piece of old canvass.

"Are these things yours?" asked the officer.

"No," I answered, very shortly and sharply.

He looked hard at me.

"Do you know to whom they do belong?"

"*No.*"

"You act curiously," he said, looking straight at me.

Just then my brother came in. He addressed the officer:

"I can't imagine to whom they belong; no one will own them."

"I think they belong to him," said the officer, indicating me.

"You are mistaken, sir," answered my brother. "I don't think he ever saw them before, any more than you or I. I will answer for him."

Upon that I sought the deck again. Shortly after, the officer with his men came out. He carried the mysterious bundle with him. When he passed me, he said in a low tone to my brother, indicating me with his eye—

"Who is that?"

"My brother."

"Why is he so insolent?"

"He thinks you have imposed upon him by taking his handkerchiefs. He has been hemming on the precious things all the passage."

"Oh, ho!" said the officer, "that's it, is it?"

At the gangway he raised the bundle in his hand.

"Now then, one and all, who owns this?"

No answer.

"It's mine, then. I wish you a good day, sir."

The latter sentence was uttered to my brother; and having uttered it, the officer descended to his boat, and the bundle went with him.

As the boat moved away, I looked after him with a bitter expression, and very uncharitable feelings. A deep sigh caused me to turn my head. The Doctor had uttered it. He, too, was looking hard at the revenue boat. I suspected the truth.

"Those things were yours, Doctor?" I said.

"Dey was." Another sigh.

"You bought them for Mrs. Brown, didn't you?" I asked, leaning towards him, and speaking in a tone which said, or was intended to say, "Be confidential with me now." But I have already said that the Doctor, when sober, was an extraordinarily discreet man. He answered me with a a melancholy smile—

"I'm tinking it don't make any difference who I bought dem for. Dey's gone now."

So saying, he sought his sanctum, the galley.

"But, Doctor," I hallooed after him, "what in thunder did you try to hide them for?"

"Cause I'se a fool!"

And he entered the galley. Poor Doctor!

On entering the cabin, I saw on the transom, a large tea chest, the lid of which was crossed by red tape, and bore upon it an official seal. There, among sundry other articles, were four of my notorious handkerchiefs. That trade had been a standing joke all the passage, and I had become so sensitive on the subject as to be ready to fight whenever it was mentioned.

At ten in the evening we were under way again, and darting up river in tow of the steamer. The pilot walked the deck all night. My brother kept him company. I made up a fire in the galley, and kept the coffee pot steaming.

Mr. Jackson, now off duty, slept at his will. The Doctor was in his berth. The watch below snored under their blankets, and the watch on deck upon their chests. The chests were below, of course, and you will call the above statement, that the watch on deck were *below*, paradoxical. Sailors understand it.

Save the pilot, my brother, the helmsman, and myself, all on board were soon in a state of unconsciousness. It was willingly permitted, because but little rest had been enjoyed by any one for two or three days.

The pilot loved a cup of coffee at any time. The night air, on this occasion, was chilly, and he had a double relish for it. I placed the sugar on a skylight, and a tray of bread beside it, and oftener than hourly, brought on the strong coffee, piping hot. In the true spirit of companionship, my brother emptied his cupfull when the pilot emptied his. I was not behindhand, and, when neither the coffee pot nor the fire required my services, joined in the measured tramp upon the deck. The pilot's heart expanded under the influence of coffee and cigars. He pointed out localities, and described them—for we could not see them in the darkness; related anecdotes, and questioned us concerning our own country.

We were happy because a long voyage was behind us, a great city just before us, and home one step nearer. So the hours of the night passed on. The fire did not go out, nor the coffee cool. The steamer groaned and smote the water in front; lights twinkled on either hand; the wind bore off the fresh smell of the land. Now and then a ship rushed past us on the opposite course, in leading strings to a strong monster of a tug, blowing out her breath of blue flame. The ports of the old Dreadnought were all lighted up—not with battle lanterns, but mild lamps, gleaming on the cots of sick men.

Ah, happy time! It is good to ascend the Thames, even by starlight. Who says the Tiber! the Tiber? I say the Thames! the Thames! Its banks are the seat of a nobler civilization, and a wider empire than Rome ever dreamed of!

With the first gleams of day we made fast to the gates of St. Catharine's Docks. An hour sufficed to make it high water, and at the expiration of that time we hauled in.

The temptation is strong upon me to tell where I went, and what I saw in this great city of London. Here the ship did not lie, as in the other ports, off the city, but *in* it, and one stride carried one from the gangway to the floor of the warehouses. Consequently, I saw much of the city. To see it was all I had to do. I ascended the spire of St. Paul's Church, and descended into the tunnel beneath the Thames. Regent's Park—— But I set out in this paragraph to make an explanation.

These Reminiscences have already exceeded all reasonable limits. To continue them would be an imposition upon those readers who, from principle, read all books through, and a piece of unpardonable stupidity in me. I shall therefore resolutely turn my back upon the temptation of which I have spoken, and make the best speed I can across the Atlantic.

July 1st the ship, now loaded with iron and chalk, was again ready for sea. When the tide served, we passed out of the dock gates. Long before night we anchored off Gravesend to receive a second visit from the officers of the custom-house—this time to *unseal*.

Just before sunset my brother, the carpenter, and myself, landed for a walk. Outside of the town the green hedges and trim, beautiful landscape filled us with admiration. This was Old England—ours was New England. The whole town seemed taking a holiday. No end of children were parading about on donkeys.

What I saw that evening has enabled me to appreciate, far better than I could otherwise have done, the surroundings of Aunt Betsy Trotwood's house at Dover, and the significance of her war-cry, "Janet, donkeys!"

The next morning we left Gravesend, and were soon out of the river.

My brother was now mate, and a Scotsman, who had come from Calcutta as hand, was second mate. This time we found the ship in good trim. She was stiff, and stood up to the wind as obstinately as we could desire. With a fine breeze we ran down the Straits of Dover. The coast along the counties of Kent and Sussex was on our right hand, and we were afforded a fine view of the "white cliffs of Albion." A railroad ran along the shore, and the soft, chalky cliffs were tunneled through in many places. We could see the locomotives with their trains, entering these tunnels, and emerging from them again.

It was well for us, we soon learned, that the ship was stiff and stood up to the wind, for we had it nearly all the time directly ahead. At length, after many days of tiresome beating, we beheld, and recognized the distinguishing features of the Gulf Stream, that river in the ocean, concerning which I had a chapter long ago. A strong north-east wind shoved us well into it, and then died away. The north-east wind had been against the set of the current, and, of course, got up a horrible, short, tumbling sea. When the wind died away, and there was nothing to steady the ship, she rolled and pitched in a way that was really wonderful. We did not, however, part a rope yarn, but a ship in sight of us pitched her fore and mizzen topgallant masts out.

August 21st our reckoning showed us to be well in with the land. When night came it was frightfully dark, and there were indications of a violent tempest. The topsails were close reefed, and under this short sail alone we headed in towards the land. The expected wind did not come, but there was lightning, and rain in excess.

This was when that terrible tornado passed through Medford, Waltham, and West Cambridge, and caused such destruction.

In the morning an old Dutch sailor was found in an empty barrel under the topgallant forecastle. When asked what he had crawled into that for, he said—

"De Blixen! Mein Gott, I dinks de end of de world pe come!"

This turbulent night was succeeded by a lovely day. When the sun rose, land was visible along the horizon to the west-north-west. All sail was made. The light air from the north freshened, and we drew rapidly in with the land, running free, and were not long in bringing Cape Ann abreast.

By the way, we were bound to Boston, which I should have stated sooner. There are some who are said to believe it is the only seaport and city in the United States, or, indeed, in America. If any think I believe so, because I did not sooner mention our port of destination, let them be undeceived—I do *not* think so.

Somewhere, the pilot came on board—I do not remember where. But I *do* remember how bright everything looked that day—objects that have since looked rough and forbidding. But if I endeavored to say to any one, How bright the water is, and how it sparkles! or, Isn't that splendid in there about Nahant!—if I undertook to make any such expressions, I say, something hard rose in my throat, and I could not articulate.

At dark the ship was fast to Battery Wharf, and the sails furled. The next morning the exodus began.

I shook hands, long and hard, with the Doctor, and wished him a happy meeting with Mrs. Brown. Then the carpenter came out of the cabin with his wallet in one hand, and a great wad of bank bills in the other; and as soon as he got these into their proper relative positions, and the whole into his pocket, he extended his honest right hand. I wrung it, and as I did so, I wished him (he blushing like a schoolgirl the while,) a speedy and happy union with *Mary*, a passenger upon whom he had been sweet. Then Joe Bacon, with hair curled, and smelling no longer of the tar bucket, but of the barber's shop, approached. We had quarrelled on the foretopsail yard the evening before, and each had promised the other, when firm footing was reached, such a thrashing as he never got before. But all this was forgotten now, and our parting bordered slightly on the touching. Lastly, young John Steward, our beau Kanaka, curled and perfumed like his white shipmate, and wearing Congress boots on his feet, and gloves on his hands, and smiles on his dusky face, came briskly up to say good-bye.

John was returned to his native Woahoo again, according to contract; but I can never believe he took kindly to old Arcadian habits again. There might have been a time when John could expend all his taste on the arrangement of his breech-clout, and took pride in wearing it, but that time was past.

There, I think those last paragraphs clean the whole thing up, and I may now safely say—imagine me making my best bow—that my REMINISCENCES OF A VOYAGE AROUND THE WORLD, are complete.

www.ingramcontent.com/pod-product-compliance
Lightning Source LLC
Chambersburg PA
CBHW021208230426
43667CB00006B/604